SAVING WYOMING'S HOBACK

Saving Wyoming's Hoback

The Grassroots Movement that Stopped
Natural Gas Development

Florence Rose Shepard and Susan L. Marsh

THE UNIVERSITY OF UTAH PRESS | SALT LAKE CITY

The Defiance House Man colophon is a registered trademark of the University of Utah Press. It is based on a four-foot-tall Ancient Puebloan pictograph (late PIII) near Glen Canyon, Utah.

21 20 19 18 17   1 2 3 4 5

Frontispiece photo of a bull moose by Susan Marsh.

Library of Congress Cataloging-in-Publication Data

Names: Shepard, Florence R. author. | Marsh, Susan (Susan L.) author.
Title: Saving Wyoming's Hoback : the grassroots movement that stopped natural gas development / Florence Rose Shepard and Susan L. Marsh.
Description: Salt Lake City : The University of Utah Press, [2017] | Includes bibliographical references and index.
Identifiers: LCCN 2016014221 | ISBN 9781607815129 (pbk. : alk. paper) | ISBN 9781607815136 (ebook)
Subjects: LCSH: Gas well drilling—Wyoming—Hoback River Watershed. | Gas well drilling—Environmental aspects—Wyoming—Hoback River Basin. | Protest movements—Wyoming—Hoback River Region.
Classification: LCC TN881.W8 S54 2017 | DDC 333.8/2330978755—dc23
LC record available at https://lccn.loc.gov/2016014221

Printed and bound in the United States of America.

CONTENTS

MAPS

PREFACE AND ACKNOWLEDGMENTS

....

OUR MOTIVATION FOR WRITING THIS BOOK was to present a case study through the eyes of many participants. Whether their involvement arose from personal interest or as part of their official duties, each person brought a heartfelt and mindful perspective to the project. We regret that time did not allow us to speak to everyone involved.

Although this book takes the form of a personal narrative from Florence's point of view, Susan was a full partner from the beginning. As a retired United States Forest Service staff officer who had been involved with energy-exploration proposals since the early 1990s, Susan brought her knowledge of the land and the complexities of public land management to telling this story.

OUR GRATITUDE AND deep appreciation go to Glenda Cotter, director of the University of Utah Press, for believing in this project and the many moments of encouragement and help she provided along the way. This book would not exist without her.

A sincere thanks to those who granted interviews, whose stories make this book what it is, and whose work helped protect the Wyoming Range: Peter Aengst, Gary Amerine, Linda Baker, Scott Bosse, Franz Camenzind, Ron and Fran Chilcote, Greg Clark, Linda Cooper, Tom Darin, Chris Deming, Lloyd Dorsey, Kniffy Hamilton, Cory Hatch, Dan Heilig, Steff Kessler, Lisa McGee, Tom Reed, Martha Saunders, Patti Smith, Dan Smitherman, Rollie Sparrowe, and Chris Wood.

Thanks to those who brought the Wyoming Range Legacy Act to fruition, including elected officials ranging from county commissioners to U.S. senators. Governor Dave Fruedenthal was an early supporter, and Governor Matt Mead took over after he was elected. The late Senator Craig Thomas formulated legislation in Congress, and Senator John Barrasso saw it through to passage. State Representative Keith Gingery and State Senator Grant Larson also lent their support at crucial moments.

Thanks to early readers of the manuscript who gave helpful comments and found errors that needed correction: Lisa McGee, Fred Swanson, Joan Degiorgio, and Dan Smitherman. We also wish to acknowledge Bridger-Teton National Forest staff for providing maps, copies of environmental documents, and press releases. John Kuzloski made a special effort to provide information when requested. Caitlin Smith, GIS contractor for the Wyoming Outdoor Council, supplied the excellent map of Wyoming Range leases that appears several times in the book.

We appreciate the ability to use photographs courtesy of EcoFlight (ecoflight.org), photographer Rita Donham of Wyoming Aero Photo (wyomingaerophoto.com), and the archives of the Murie Center (muriecenter.org).

Most of all, our thanks to all whose tireless work on behalf of the Wyoming Range resulted in the win-win decision that saved this unique environment.

GLOSSARY OF ACRONYMS

....

BLM	Bureau of Land Management	NGO	nongovernmental organizations
BTNF	Bridger-Teton National Forest	NOLS	National Outdoor Leadership School
CCC	Civilian Conservation Corps	OPEC	Organization of Petroleum Exporting Countries
CEO	chief executive officer		
CFWR	Citizens for the Wyoming Range	PAWG	Pinedale Anticline Working Group
CPWR	Citizens Protecting the Wyoming Range	PXP	Plains Exploration & Production Company
DEIS	draft environmental impact statement		
DFC	desired future conditions	RARE	roadless area review and evaluation
EIS	environmental impact statement	SDSBT	Stop Drilling—Save the Bridger-Teton
GYC	Greater Yellowstone Coalition	TPL	Trust for Public Land
IBLA	Interior Board of Land Appeals	TU	Trout Unlimited
KOLAB	Kemmerer Outdoor Laboratory	TWS	The Wilderness Society
MA	management area	USFS	United States Forest Service
NEPA	National Environmental Policy Act of 1970	USFWS	United States Fish and Wildlife Service
		WOC	Wyoming Outdoor Council
NFMA	National Forest Management Act of 1976	WRLA	Wyoming Range Legacy Act

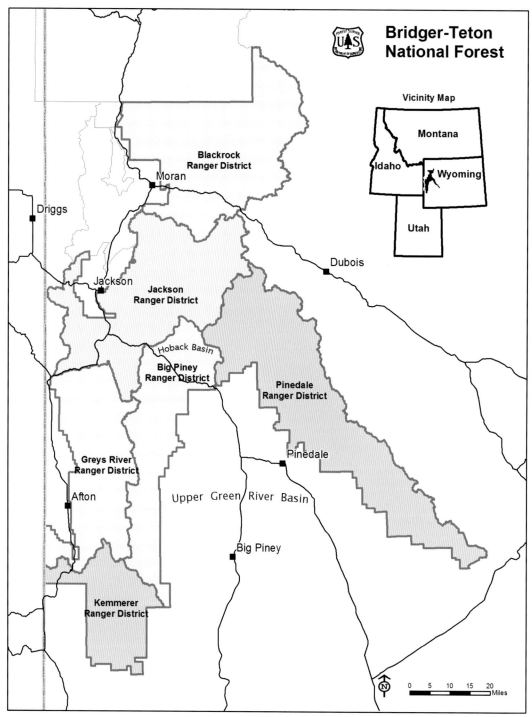

Bridger-Teton National Forest

Vicinity Map

Montana

Idaho

Wyoming

Utah

Blackrock
Ranger District

Moran

Driggs

Dubois

Jackson

Jackson
Ranger District

Hoback Basin

Big Piney
Ranger District

Pinedale
Ranger District

Greys River
Ranger District

Pinedale

Afton

Upper Green River Basin

Big Piney

Kemmerer
Ranger District

0   5   10   15   20
Miles

N

MAP 1. The Bridger-Teton National Forest (BTNF), Wyoming,
showing the areas discussed in this book. Map courtesy of
the USFS.

1

We Did It!

OCTOBER 4, 2012. SUSAN AND I FOUND SEATS in the auditorium at Snow King Mountain Resort in Jackson Hole, Wyoming, where we joined about one hundred others waiting for the meeting to begin. In the group were individuals who, at key moments in the past, had shown extraordinary will and expertise in carrying forward an effort to stop the Plains Exploration & Production Company (PXP), which held mineral leases within the Bridger-Teton National Forest (BTNF), from exploring and drilling up to 136 gas wells in the Noble Basin, part of Wyoming's Hoback Basin. Unchallenged, natural-gas drilling and development in the northeastern Wyoming Range would have industrialized the area and brought with it water and air pollution and a complete change in the character of the landscape and its human communities. Now, as we waited in our seats at Snow King, the crowd buzzed with anticipation: rumors had been circulating that the Trust for Public Land had negotiated a buyout of the leases. The rumors, as it turned out, were true.

Those gathered to celebrate the successful conclusion of this long struggle represented a diverse group of people: hunters and anglers, backcountry ramblers, ranchers, big game outfitters, businessmen and women, conservationists and environmentalists, union members, and elected officials that spanned from county commissioners to Wyoming's governor. After years of effort to prevent gas drilling in the Hoback Basin, supporters were filled with a sense of jubilation and perhaps a touch of disbelief. Most of those present, if asked five years earlier, would have said changing the outcome was impossible, for PXP held valid rights to the leases, and their horse was long out of the barn. Preventing drilling seemed to be an impossible dream that only a few stalwart souls had held to tenaciously from the beginning.

How did it happen? How did a varied group of individuals with important insight, information, and resources join at critical times to help overcome obstacles that had arisen during the previous decade? The tremendous unity of purpose displayed by residents of the Hoback Basin, led

FIGURE 1. Hoback Peak stands in the distance while fall's colors cloak the foothills along the upper Hoback River. Hoback Peak, at 10,862 feet, is the highest landmark in the Grayback Roadless Area. Photo by Susan Marsh.

initially by a few conservation-minded people, convinced philanthropists that the effort to stop the drilling was well-conceived and supported by the community. Different in class, ideologies, and professions, citizens were bonded by a single incorruptible intuition: a shared sense of the integrity and uniqueness of the Hoback Basin in the Wyoming Range. And they were united in their determination to defend it.

In a sort of relay race, the baton passed from one coalition to another for almost a decade. With each effort, momentum built as plans became more focused and effective and the threat of potential energy development became clearer.

THE RUSH OF energy development that washed over Wyoming beginning in the mid-1990s is not a new phenomenon in this region. Through repeated cycles since the turn of the twentieth century, Wyoming communities have experienced the "boom-and-bust" stages of energy development. The boom phase begins with the need for a labor force to build the infrastructure for producing and transporting products. Businesses in small towns expand, and new enterprises and motels spring up in response to the need for housing and services. Often "man camps"— temporary housing developments set apart from the small towns—are established to accommodate nonlocal workers. These isolated compounds make few allowances for families, leisure, or recreation and give their residents little sense of being part of a larger community. New revenue flowing into the town and county, while welcome, is rarely enough to cover the social services, schools, police, and medical facilities that often become exhausted.

Once the necessary infrastructure has been completed, however, fewer employees are needed to run and maintain the energy facilities. Temporary workers are laid off, and the small town enters the bust phase of the cycle: businesses

suffer, and the economy in general becomes depressed.

The era after World War II, when the demand for electricity and fuel for mechanization soared, is an example of this boom-and-bust cycle. Strip coal mines opened on huge tracts of land, fueling enormous power plants around the state. Just as communities adjusted to accommodate the influx of construction workers, the project-development stage ended, and only a fraction of the labor force needed to build the energy-producing installations remained to monitor them. The communities went into local depressions as new housing, hotels, and food services were no longer needed.

A similar cycle occurred in the 1960s when gas fields were developed in the Green River Basin on the east flank of the Wyoming Range and companies began building pipelines across southwestern Wyoming to deliver products to large distribution centers. By the 1970s, derelict pump stations and holding tanks were left to rust, becoming a permanent blight on the landscape. Unfortunately, institutional memory in small communities falters when dollar signs appear. The extent of the consequences of a bust phase is difficult to anticipate and easy to ignore.

The boom phase of energy development during the 1990s took people in the upper Green River Basin by surprise. The changes happened quickly, and few people were prepared for the scale and extent of the ensuing development. Within a decade, 642 new gas wells were drilled within the Pinedale Anticline, accompanied by nearly 200 miles of road and 128 miles of pipeline. The consequences of rapid, large-scale energy development in the Green River Basin, just a few miles east of Hoback Basin, brought home the reality of what might happen if PXP's leases went into full field development.

The Pinedale Anticline's 198,000 acres of sagebrush steppe habitat in the Green River Basin are 80 percent federally owned and contain one

FIGURE 2. An aerial view of Jonah Field in the upper Green River Basin. The number of oil wells, drill pads, roads, and pipelines increases every year. Photo by Bruce Gordon, courtesy of EcoFlight.

FIGURE 3. The facilities associated with gas production in the upper Green River Basin are large and extensive. Photo by Bruce Gordon, courtesy of EcoFlight.

of the richest concentrations of natural gas in the United States, currently estimated at more than twenty-five trillion cubic feet.[1] They are also home to significant mule deer and sage grouse populations and serve as transitory habitat and migration routes for other species, including pronghorn, elk, and moose. Since the beginning of energy extraction, the number of sage grouse and mule deer has declined, in some years by more than 60 percent.[2] The effect of development on pronghorn is also beginning to be felt.

Although this is of great concern, the current amount of development mitigation is not sufficient to reverse the downward trend, and the future of wildlife populations remains uncertain. The value of this wildlife, which evolved within its unique ecological niche, cannot be measured in dollars and cents—it is irreplaceable and thus priceless.

Hydraulic fracturing (fracking), a process by which pressurized water and chemicals are pumped underground into rock strata to release hydrocarbons, was implemented in this area and boosted production to all time highs. Air pollution and contamination of water sources became problems as a result. Although the energy companies could have used the Jonah and Pinedale Anticline fields as an example of careful extraction and sensitivity to preserving the ecological health of the region, unsound methods of drilling magnified the detrimental impacts to the extent that some appear to be irreversible. The upper Green River Basin, with the rugged Wind River Range as its scenic backdrop, once had some of the cleanest air in the country. Now, when temperature inversions trap stagnant air during the winter, the ozone level rises, and haze often fills the basin.

The bad press on fracking was also in the spotlight when the PXP project was proposed and—added to the increase in pollution and decrease in wildlife populations—was another

FIGURE 4. Gas flares from a well in the Green River Basin north of Pinedale. While this kind of pollution has been reduced in recent years, ozone, particulates, and oxides of nitrogen remain a major concern. Photo by William Belveal, courtesy of the Upper Green River Valley Coalition.

factor that helped unify the movement against gas drilling in the Hoback Basin.

THE STORY OF the environmental victory in the Hoback Basin is convoluted. To understand it fully requires fundamental knowledge about federal land-management agencies, their mission, and the laws enacted to allow exploration and development of mineral resources while also protecting the environment. The proper development and utilization of resources on public lands has been an ongoing issue for the federal government since the western expansion began with President Thomas Jefferson in the early nineteenth century. A common purpose of government agencies from the beginning was to encourage settlement and private ownership of this vast expanse through farming and personal enterprise.

Before a century had passed, conservationists, who appreciated the unfettered natural environment, became alarmed by the rapid depletion of forest lands. Acts and policies were initiated with nominal effect until the end of the nineteenth century, when the excesses of timbering and watershed degradation had become obvious. On June 4, 1897, the first national forest reserves were created, including many large parcels in the Rocky Mountains. In 1905, through the efforts of Gifford Pinchot, the United States Forest Service (USFS) was established to manage and protect these timbered lands. It took until 1946, however, to create a comparable federal agency—the Bureau of Land Management (BLM)—to watch over rangeland being destroyed by drought and overgrazing. The Multiple-Use Sustained-Yield Act of 1960 gave further direction to the USFS, stating that "the national forests are established and shall be administered for outdoor recreation, range, timber, watershed, and wildlife and fish purposes."[3]

The act, however, specifically stated that mineral resources were excluded from the jurisdiction of the USFS, a Department of Agriculture agency. Instead, the Department of the Interior was responsible for these resources. Thus, because the BLM was a Department of the Interior agency, it became responsible for energy leasing within the national forests. As a result, surface resources are managed by one set of laws and regulations, while mineral resources (including energy) are subject to different and, sometimes, conflicting ones.

During the 1960s and '70s, a number of environmental laws were passed that are relevant to this story. The Clean Water Act, Clean Air Act, Wild and Scenic Rivers Act, Endangered Species Act, and the Wilderness Act, which resulted in agencies conducting an inventory of potential wilderness, or roadless areas, all contributed. Two laws—the National Environmental Policy Act (NEPA) of 1970 and the National Forest Management Act (NFMA) of 1976, which set forest planning into motion—are especially important because they require the USFS to determine which areas within the national forests are suitable for energy exploration and drilling. The agency must also review development plans by energy companies on national forest land to ensure compliance with environmental regulations. Finally, both NEPA and NFMA require public participation at several stages of forest planning and project review.

One must also be aware of the procedure for issuing mineral leases on public lands to understand the PXP scenario. Beginning with President Thomas Jefferson, the government encouraged private ownership of western lands. Squatters were commonly accepted and were often given the opportunity to purchase tracts of land at reasonable prices. Land was also sold at nominal prices for homesteading or mineral extraction. At first, those people who purchased government lands also received the mineral rights. Then the General Mining Act of 1872, which applied to hard-rock mining, established the historical precedent of issuing mineral leases apart from ownership.

The Mineral Leasing Act of 1920 clarified the right of the federal government to lease energy resources, such as coal, petroleum, and natural gas, and minerals, such as phosphate, sodium, sulfur, and potassium. After the BLM was established in 1946, it became the principal administrator of this leasing process, even for other federal lands. The federal government retains ownership of the mineral resources, which can then be offered to private companies to lease. However, even though the underground mineral resource has been leased, the USFS or BLM retains above-the-ground land management. This arrangement, where one party holds surface rights—in this case, a federal agency—and another holds the right to develop underground resources is referred to as a split estate. Where the land is privately held, either an individual entity (the energy company) or the federal government may control the mineral estate.

Mineral leases on public lands carry stipulations required by the agency. These are intended to assure that the federal forests and rangelands that must continue serving multiple purposes for the public do not receive irreparable damage. The stipulations are an inherent part of federal mineral supervision and continue to apply, no matter how many times the leases are traded to various private interests.

The USFS and the BLM share responsibility for issuing mineral leases within national forests. The USFS determines which tracts of land—within areas already slated as "available" for energy development as part of the forest plan—will be offered. With the consent of the USFS, the BLM sets dates and auctions the leases. Each agency is then responsible for approving the detailed plans of companies that want to explore and develop energy resources, which must follow NEPA mandates: to protect the natural environment, identify possible negative impact, and present adequate mitigation plans for any harmful effects to the ecosystem.

The roles of the USFS and the BLM in managing leased oil and gas resources are defined by a section of the Code of Federal Regulations, a weighty tome covering a wide range of regulations developed by the government to implement laws passed by Congress. Within national forest lands, the USFS has the full responsibility and authority to approve and regulate all surface-disturbing activities associated with oil and gas exploration and, through environmental analysis, reaches a decision on approving a company's development plan.

At this point, the USFS may propose potential mitigation measures. The USFS decision typically specifies road access, temporary and buried pipeline routes, other facilities, and design criteria for the project. Within the same lands, the BLM regulates all "down-hole" operations as well as directly related surface activities. The BLM reviews and

approves a drilling plan, which then can become part of a master development plan for the project.

When the BLM approves this plan, it in effect approves all subsequent applications to drill from the company unless the anticipated impact is greater than those detailed in the initial NEPA analysis. Therefore, any environmental concerns or needs for mitigation must come to the attention of the USFS prior to approval of the master plan. This convoluted approval process, while legally designed to allow public involvement, often leaves the public in its dust. Approval can take years, and public notice may consist of little more than a small entry in the back pages of a newspaper.

The NEPA process is straightforward, if properly followed. When a drilling proposal is made, the responsible land-management agency prepares a scoping document, which outlines the proposal, its purpose, the need for action, and a list of preliminary issues. Staff specialists and members of the public are invited to comment on the proposal and provide any additional concerns. The nature and location of the project determine what level of analysis is required. If no special circumstances exist (the presence of a threatened species, for example) and anticipated impact can be mitigated, the agency conducts an environmental assessment and publishes a Decision Note Finding of No Significant Impact.

If special circumstances or potential effects that cannot be adequately mitigated are expected, the agency must prepare an environmental impact statement (EIS) that discloses them. The record of decision that accompanies the EIS may either allow the project with alterations that better protect resources or deny it. Most often the project is allowed with these protective changes. The public is invited to review and comment on any of these documents. In the case of highly controversial projects requiring an EIS, public meetings or hearings may be convened to allow feedback. A final EIS follows, and in cases where the analysis is shown to be flawed after the process has been completed, a supplemental EIS may be necessary.

THE BTNF DETERMINED through its forest plan (published in 1990) that much of the Wyoming Range was potentially available for leasing. The forest plan included standard stipulations as well as special ones for certain parts of the forest. The BLM issued some leases within the BTNF in the mid-1990s, and minor exploration and development occurred.

The term for a lease is ten years; after that, it expires unless it is renewed or issued to a different company. A group of the Hoback Basin leases issued in 1993 and 1994 was about to expire in 2004, when PXP acquired them.

Much had changed in the social and environmental milieu: the country was at war in Iraq and Afghanistan, and energy resources were of great strategic value. A decade of energy development had transformed the upper Green River Basin. People in the Hoback Basin had become alarmed by this rapid industrialization of the landscape that seemed poised to move their way.

Several events also occurred in 2004 that raised the awareness of citizens in general and sportspeople, outfitters, ranchers, and conservation groups in particular. One incident in particular brought citizens to their feet. The BTNF announced its intention to consider leasing for energy development 175,000 acres in the Wyoming Range that the forest plan had identified as available. A broad constituency of citizens, conservation organizations, and elected officials, including Governor Dave Freudenthal, Senator Craig Thomas, and State Senator Grant Larson, were concerned and objected to the size of the proposal.

In response, the BTNF reduced the original consideration to 44,720 acres, mostly within parcels that already had roads, scattered from the settlement of Merna on Horse Creek down the eastern flank of the Wyoming Range to Deadline Ridge. Citizens then objected to issuing any leases in this area because baseline scientific data were not available and the environmental impact had not been adequately studied.

Nonetheless, the USFS authorized the BLM to proceed with four different lease sales between December 2005 and August 2006. Citizens protested these sales to the BLM, citing numerous circumstances that had changed since the USFS made the initial leasing decisions in the early 1990s: degraded air quality, the reduction of a local mule deer herd, and the listing of Canada lynx as a federally protected threatened species. The BLM denied the protests and proceeded with the first two sales, relying on the judgment of the USFS, the surface land manager that had consented to leasing these areas. Many of these same citizens then called on the Interior Board of Land Appeals (IBLA), a federal review board whose purpose is to settle these disagreements. The IBLA granted a stay on development of these leases and indicated that the citizen-appellants would likely be successful because of the merits of their appeals.

When the final two of the four lease sales occurred later in 2006, the number of protests, including one from Governor Dave Freudenthal, increased. Citing the IBLA's stay decisions on the first two lease sales, the BLM upheld the protests on these final two, which placed the leases in a pending category.

What happened with the 44,720 acres alerted the public to the many pitfalls of mineral leasing within national forests. The prospect of industrial development along the eastern flank of the Wyoming Range unified citizen advocates, raised awareness, and solidified resolve to protect public lands for activities other than energy development. This series of leases played an important

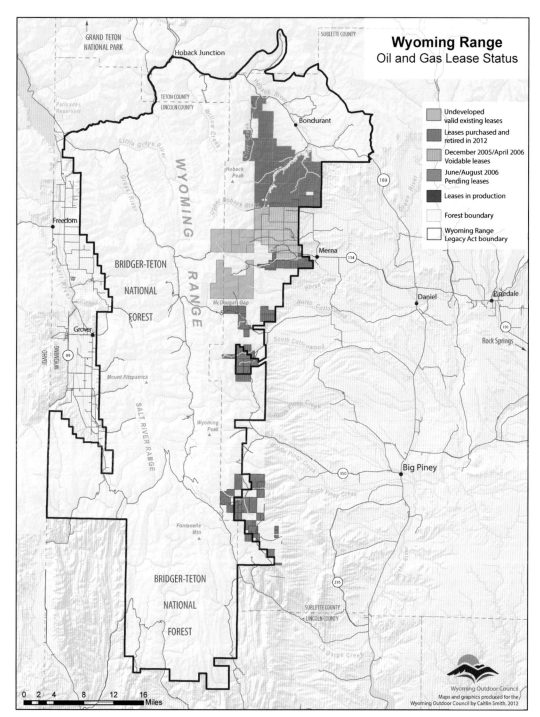

MAP 2. Existing valid leases along the eastern front of the Wyoming Range totaling 44,720 acres. The controversy over these leases was instrumental in gaining support for the Wyoming Range Legacy Act. Map by Caitlin Smith, courtesy of the Wyoming Outdoor Council.

role in the public response to the PXP project, as well as efforts to protect the Wyoming Range as a whole. At the time this book went to press, the BTNF had updated its draft supplemental EIS to consider 39,490 acres. The preferred alternative was to withdraw consent to lease. The final decision is expected in January 2017.

ENTER ANOTHER PIECE of legislation: the Wyoming Range Legacy Act. Beginning in 2006, a coalition of citizens, sports groups, and conservation organizations have worked tirelessly to protect a little-known, but priceless, wildland resource in remote, rural Wyoming. As concern over the possible outcome of leasing 44,720 acres on the margins of the Wyoming Range grew, outfitters, sportspeople, ranchers, and conservation groups began a campaign to protect the entire area and lobbied Senator Craig Thomas, who had long served in office and been chair of the powerful Committee on Energy and Natural Resources.

Senator Thomas, a consistently conservative politician concerned about fiscal responsibility of government (to the extent that he repeatedly voted against his own party's budget, much to the consternation of his Republican colleagues) and in favor of energy development in Wyoming, also deeply appreciated the Wyoming Range and its special qualities. He wished to leave a legacy for the state and worked to fund a new pathway in Grand Teton National Park to accommodate hikers and bicyclists. He looked at potential additions to the Wild and Scenic Rivers system in the headwaters of the Snake River, which included the Hoback River. And he was interested in protecting the Wyoming Range from the effects of industrialization that had transformed the upper Green River Basin.

In 2004, Kniffy Hamilton, then supervisor of the BTNF, invited Senator Thomas on a pack trip into the Wyoming Range to see some of the large acreage the USFS was considering for energy development. After visiting the upper Hoback River and Roosevelt Meadows, the senator was convinced that certain special places should not be leased.

On the heels of Senator Thomas's pack trip, *Wind River Wilderness,* edited by Ron Chilcote, was published. Through beautiful photographs and essays, the large-format book portrayed the backcountry and mountains in northwestern Wyoming. Distributed to all congressional members at this critical historical moment, the book raised awareness of a region that needed to be protected.

Unfortunately, Senator Thomas died before he could introduce his bills on the Wyoming Range and the Snake River tributaries to Congress. John Barrasso was appointed to fill out his term. After holding town meetings throughout the state to get a sense of the public's sentiments regarding Senator Thomas's planned legislation, Senator Barrasso spearheaded the amended Craig Thomas Snake Headwaters Legacy Act and the Wyoming Range Legacy Act as part of the Omnibus Public Land Management Act of 2008, signed in early 2009 by President Obama.

The Craig Thomas Snake Headwaters Legacy Act amended the Wild and Scenic Rivers Act to include more than four hundred miles in the Snake River watershed. The Wyoming Range Legacy Act protected 1.2 million acres of the Wyoming Range from future gas and oil leases while honoring existing mineral leases. Coming when it did, the Wyoming Range Legacy Act provided needed ballast to support citizen efforts to find a solution to concerns about PXP's drilling proposal. It also raised hopes for a favorable outcome regarding the contested 44,720 acres.

The legislation was seen as the best chance to limit future energy leasing within the national forest. Many of those who worked to see the Wyoming Range Legacy Act signed into law were convinced that drilling on valid existing leases could

FIGURE 5. Dedication ceremony for the passage of the Wyoming Range Legacy Act, held at Gary Amerine's outfitting camp at Greys River. Senator John Barrasso, Susan Thomas, and Gary Amerine *(left to right)* pose beside a new sign. Photo courtesy of the BTNF.

not be prevented, however. "It's a done deal," they said, and their conclusion seemed logical.

The coalition that had worked for years to protect the Wyoming Range split when it came time to address PXP's development proposal. Some individuals and organizations felt they had done what they set out to do with passage of the legislation. Others resisted the idea of allowing the company, even if it held valid mineral leases, to operate on a business-as-usual basis. The second group, including the Wyoming Outdoor Council (WOC) and the Wilderness Society (TWS), worked with Citizens for the Wyoming Range (CFWR) to challenge the assumed inevitability of a gas field in the Noble Basin.

Their strategy was two part: assuming PXP proceeded with the project, they would try to make sure it became the most highly regulated gas field in Wyoming, subject to stringent "best-management practices" based on current technology and standards. They referred to this as a "gold standard" for environmental protection. The second strategy involved pushing the USFS to enforce all forest plan standards, stipulations, and best-management practices, hoping it would make PXP abandon the project due to its high

THE HOBACK RIVER: HEART OF THE BASIN

From its headwaters near 10,862-foot Hoback Peak, the Hoback River tumbles through rugged mountain landscape, gathering strength and volume from tributaries along the way.

The river's uppermost seven miles are eligible for wild river status, and parts of its tributaries, Shoal and Granite Creeks, are already designated as wild and scenic.

Shoal Creek, a national wild river. Photo: Susan Marsh

cost. Perhaps PXP would then be willing to negotiate a buyout and retire the leases.

The Wyoming Range Legacy Act was the key to the possibility of a buyout. Without it, there would have been nothing to prevent the USFS/BLM from issuing new leases in the future, and potential donors to a buyout would not have been interested without the guarantee that these areas would never be leased again.

Residents of a large subdivision called Hoback Ranches realized that the proposed PXP development could, among other things, jeopardize their water source. Other enclaves of people living in the Hoback Basin had another primary concern. In this basin surrounded by high mountains, air pollution would collect, unable to dissipate due to narrow Hoback Canyon downstream. Most importantly, all of the residents of the Hoback

FIGURE 6. Spring elk migration in the Wyoming Range follows well-worn trails. Elk, mule deer, and pronghorn are among the species that migrate into the Hoback Basin in spring, rear their young in the high country, and move on to winter ranges in the fall. Photo: Susan Marsh.

Basin agreed that the PXP project would destroy one of the most important habitats for wild game in the United States and disrupt historic migratory routes.

As the campaign to stop the PXP project gained momentum, two grassroots groups formed: Stop Drilling—Save the Bridger-Teton (SDSBT) and CFWR. They joined with regional and national conservation organizations, including TWS and the WOC to inform the public about the status of events. The catch phrase "Too Special to Drill" was on the lips of many people.

In December of 2010, the draft EIS (DEIS) for the PXP project was published. A small group of outfitters, sportspeople, and ranchers, together with Governor Freudenthal, negotiated a plan with PXP that they called the Wyoming Range Conservation and Noble Basin Development

FIGURE 7. Jack Creek and the East Rim of the Hoback Basin. This is a prime area for hunting, fishing, and outfitting. Photo: Susan Marsh.

Agreement. This agreement allowed development of gas fields in the Noble Basin while providing for off-site mitigation funds and retiring some nearby leases that PXP held. It was intended to reduce the effects of development and protect other parts of the Wyoming Range, where PXP held leases it was willing to relinquish.

It never took effect, partly because controversy developed over its provisions and the way the negotiations were conducted. However, it was one approach to solving a pressing problem that this particular segment of citizens agreed was the only solution. To the credit of those who negotiated it, they did no harm and, in fact, contributed to final success. Through their public-relations campaign, they shone a spotlight on the danger of drilling in Noble Basin and thus helped to garner support to protect it.

Meantime, WOC, TWS, and CFWR formalized a plan to solicit comments on the DEIS from local and national constituencies, encouraging anyone concerned with the Wyoming Range to respond. More than sixty thousand comments were submitted and documented. Most of them objected to the PXP proposal for drilling. Objections focused on a number of deficiencies within the EIS, pointed out by experts with an eye for such things, and citizens requested that a supplemental EIS be drafted to correct these problems. The BTNF announced in November 2011 that it would prepare a supplemental EIS.

By this time, the Trust for Public Land was already negotiating a buyout. Interested philanthropists, encouraged by broad public support and the increasing notoriety of the Wyoming Range, stepped forward. The generosity of these philanthropists made the buyout feasible. Historically in the United States, philanthropy has been a willing partner with citizens and the federal government in the effort to protect unique habitats and sites. Agencies and citizens often lack the financial means to broker buyouts that involve millions of dollars. National and city parks, forests, seaside and desert nature preserves, and a great many other significant environmental and historic sites have been saved through the contributions of philanthropists. This was also the case with the PXP buyout.

The buyout, as a way of saying no to gas drilling, succeeded for many reasons. The astute organizers of the campaign garnered the support of the small local community as well as a national constituency. The example of development in the Pinedale Anticline and Jonah Field in the upper Green River Basin loomed large as a probable outcome and undoubtedly helped cement opposition to drilling in the Hoback Basin. The prospect was clear: with drilling, the basin would lose its clean air and water.

The most important factor that united residents against the drilling may have been psychological. The late Paul Shepard once said, "You can't know who you are until you know where you are." The citizens of Hoback Basin knew who they were and were firmly grounded. Some had been born and raised in the area and were following in the footsteps of ancestral homesteaders. Most, however, had made the choice to live in the basin with its healthy and rugged ambience. A primary reason for the remarkable unity against drilling may have been deeply subjective as well as pragmatic.

AT THE CROWDED meeting at Snow King in October 2012, Deb Love, representing the Trust for Public Land, stepped up to the podium.

"Today," she said, "I have great pleasure to announce that after six months of negotiations, the Trust for Public Land has reached an agreement with PXP for the purchase of roughly 58,000 acres of federal oil and gas leases in the Hoback."

Thunderous applause, sighs of relief, a few tears.

Governor Matt Mead followed. "This is an outstanding outcome for the people of Wyoming, a true win-win resolution," he said. Tall and determined, Susan Thomas, wife of the late U.S. Senator Craig Thomas, spoke of her husband's dedication to this unique area when he began authoring the Wyoming Range Legacy Act in 2007, an important element in the favorable outcome we were celebrating.

Deb Love concluded by explaining that the buyout of leases would cost $8.75 million, to be raised by December 31. She acknowledged that more than half that amount had already been committed by philanthropists, but about $2 million more were needed to finalize the buyout. The Trust for Public Land initiated a campaign to raise the funds by announcing that each person could save one acre of land in Noble Basin for $150. Foundations, organizations, and citizens also worked to raise the money, and contributions began streaming in. Meetings, concerts, and fund-raisers were organized in Jackson Hole and Bondurant to sustain the momentum. A thousand residents and nonresidents—ranchers who used the Wyoming Range for grazing their livestock, hunters, anglers, campers, and hikers—who had written letters opposing the drilling, sent donations. This commitment on the part of ordinary citizens demonstrated their dedication to maintaining the ecological integrity of Noble Basin.

On January 2, 2013, the Trust for Public Land announced that the drilling leases had been acquired from PXP and, after due process, would be turned over to the USFS and retired—forever.

2

The Hoback

AS I CROSS THE RIM ON A DRIVE BACK TO MY cabin, the familiar silhouettes of mountains surrounding the Hoback Basin come into view. Since childhood, when I first visited the area on a family vacation, the rugged beauty of this place has filled me with wonder. Of necessity when driving, I focus my attention on the circuitous road that works its way down the mountain through evergreen forests, aspen groves, and sagebrush foothills. Sometimes, to my delight, the dark head of a moose appears above the willows just off the highway along Fisherman Creek. One last sweeping curve, and I enter the valley floor of what we residents fondly call the Hoback. The generic "Hoback" refers to the Hoback Basin, the Hoback Range, and the Hoback River.

Twenty minutes is all it takes to drive the twenty miles through the Hoback Basin. Summer travelers with their minds set on the vistas of Grand Teton and Yellowstone National Parks may find nothing extraordinary about this place. The same is not true for residents. The Hoback is the backdrop of their existence, and they are always aware of the nuances of the landscape that defines this place. This amalgam of geography and cultural history is what shaped the context for the diverse constituency who joined to save the Hoback from gas drilling and industrialization.

WHEN LOCAL FOLKS refer to the Hoback, they are not so much thinking of a geographic location but the focal point of many meanings. Nonetheless, the Hoback does lie at the heart of expanding rings of identifiable regions: Sublette County, the Wyoming Range, the BTNF, the Greater Yellowstone Bioregion, Wyoming, the Rocky Mountains, the United States, and North America. However, the Hoback is much more than a series of geopolitical locations.

On a 3-D relief map, the Hoback Basin is only a thumbprint pressed into mountainous terrain. The Gros Ventre Range borders it to the north with peaks rising to 11,682 feet. To the west, the Hoback Range, most of it well above 10,000 feet, stands against the sky, a northeasterly offshoot of the larger Wyoming Range. The Rim, which

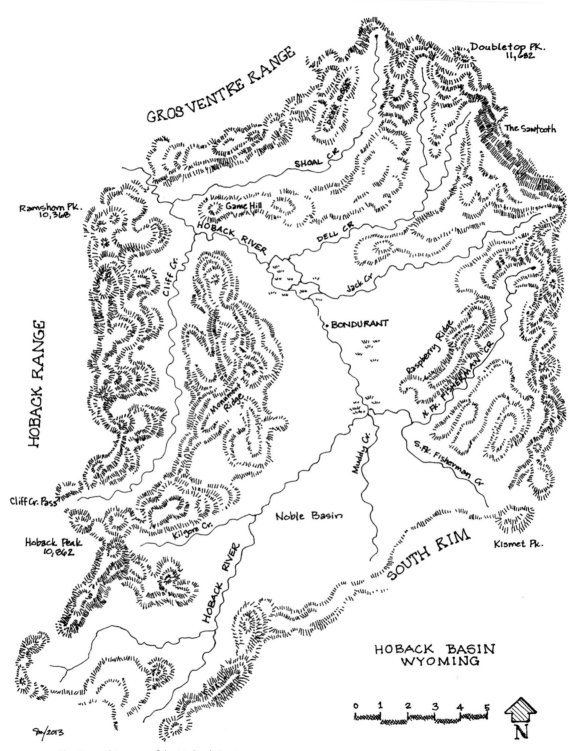

GROS VENTRE RANGE

Doubletop Pk.
11,682

The Sawtooth

Deer Ridge

SHOAL CR.

Ramshorn Pk.
10,368

Game Hill

HOBACK RIVER

DELL CR.

Jack Cr.

HOBACK RANGE

Cliff Cr.

BONDURANT

Raspberry Ridge

N. Fk. FISHERMAN CR.

Monument Ridge

S. Fk. Fisherman Cr.

Muddy Cr.

Cliff Cr. Pass

Kilgore Cr.

Noble Basin

SOUTH RIM

Kismet Pk.

Hoback Peak
10,862

HOBACK RIVER

HOBACK BASIN
WYOMING

0 1 2 3 4 5

N

SM/2013

MAP 3. Physiographic map of the Hoback Basin, upper Hoback River, and surrounding mountains. Map courtesy of Susan Marsh.

divides the Hoback and the upper Green River Basin to the east, completes this circle of high country.

The geologic processes that created this region began during a period of mountain building and tectonic movement known as the Laramide orogeny some seventy to eighty million years ago. Great forces pushed the Pacific and North American plates together and caused layers of rock to shear into massive sheets that overrode others in a series of thrust faults. The Wyoming Range is part of the continent-long region known as the Overthrust Belt, some of which contains rich reserves of hydrocarbons.[1]

The Hoback Range displays classic Overthrust Belt topography: tilted sedimentary layers with dip slopes on the west and cliff faces on the east. Exposed bedrock includes some Paleozoic limestone and sandstone as well as a sequence of Triassic through Tertiary sediments, some of which are stained rust red by iron oxide and are relatively unconsolidated, and therefore easily eroded. During thunderstorms in summer months, the runoff in Jamb and Kilgore Creeks turns the Hoback River brick red, much to the frustration of anglers. The Hoback Range also experienced Pleistocene glaciation, but subsequent erosion has muted most of the glacial features.

The Gros Ventre Range was formed by high-angle block faulting, rather than thrust faults. Thick layers of sedimentary rock were pushed up and fractured by pressure from deep crustal movement. As they sheared, the mountains continued to rise while the land on the basin side of the fault subsided. As you hike to the headwaters of Granite and Shoal Creeks in the Gros Ventres, you walk back in time into Precambrian metamorphic rocks that form the crystalline core of these mountains. They underlie the sedimentary layers and are more resistant to erosion. These canyons display the classic U-shaped profile of valleys formed by glaciers, which retreated from the Gros Ventre Range

about twelve thousand years ago. As the glaciers receded, the erosional forces of gravity, water, and wind continued to sculpt the present contours.

The Eocene Pass Peak Formation, a layer of sandstone and conglomerate resistant to erosion, is exposed in outcrops in the foothills around the periphery of the Hoback Basin and on the summit of Clark Butte. It forms a divide on the eastern edge of the Hoback Basin called The Rim, a forested highland that separates the watershed of the Hoback River from the Green/Colorado River drainage. Waters on the east side of The Rim flow south into the Green and Colorado Rivers, eventually reaching the Sea of Cortez. On the west side of The Rim, water drains into the Snake/Columbia River watershed that empties into the Pacific Ocean.

Because of its diverse geomorphology and erosional features, the Hoback Basin is a spectacular landscape with bare, steep bedrock slopes, waterfalls, deep glacial canyons, and caves. Wildflowers dominate the area in July and August, and aspens turn gold in the fall.

From its headwaters on 10,862-foot Hoback Peak, the Hoback River tumbles through rugged terrain, gathering strength and volume from springs, seeps, and tributaries along the way. Small streams form a network that sustains native fish and a healthy ecosystem.

The Hoback River and its tributaries have sculpted a series of gentle valleys reaching down from the high mountains. Between them stand midelevation ridges; 8,257-foot Monument Ridge is the most prominent. Fortress Hill and Raspberry Ridge form another long promontory to the northeast. Between them a series of draws and creeks and basins creates a diverse landscape for both wildlife and people. Separated by erosion, Clarke Butte, once a part of these ridges, now stands alone northwest of my cabin.

Finally finding level ground on the floor of the basin, the Hoback River slows and meanders

MOUNTAIN-MAKING BEDROCK

The glaciated fault-block mountains of the Gros Ventres with their underlying crystalline core, differ from the younger sedimentary rocks of the Wyoming Range, which typifies the Overthrust Belt in topography, geologic structure, and the presence of hydrocarbon-bearing rocks.

An erratic block left by a glacier on a terrace near Granite Creek. Photo: Susan Marsh.

as it scribes a great arc before heading west into narrow Hoback Canyon. There it has cut a path between the Wyoming and Gros Ventre Ranges, where the two collided eons ago. The highway follows the river's winding path, and one can view the geological formations of two different mountain ranges. This unusual canyon delights geologists, rock climbers, hikers, and kayakers in the summer. In the winter, travelers must watch for avalanches that may block the road.

FIGURE 8. In Hoback Canyon, the river leaves the wide basin upstream and carves a deep gorge between the Wyoming and Gros Ventre Ranges. Photo: Susan Marsh.

The surrounding mountainsides offer diverse vegetation: spring-saturated hillsides that support willows, bog birch, and other water-loving plants; extensive aspen stands, wildflower parks, sagebrush meadows, and montane forest. The highest elevations are within the true alpine zone, above 10,500 feet.

The floor of the Hoback Basin, at 6,500 feet and higher, consists of sagebrush steppe and meadows along the Hoback River, some of which were cleared of sagebrush by early homesteaders. They flooded the area to kill the sagebrush and then grubbed out the roots, often by hand.

TODAY THE HOBACK Basin and its surrounding mountainsides offer diverse habitat for wild flora and fauna that please ranchers, outfitters, nature lovers, and summer residents like me. In the early 1800s, the western frontier offered opportunities for new land and resources for development by yeoman farmers, religious sects, and enterprising persons. Many people in crowded cities and those on failed farms were ready for a new beginning. The United States extended its borders to 2.3 billion acres in just sixty-four years, and more than two-thirds of that land lay west of the Mississippi River.[2]

The government's primary goal during expansion, beginning with President Jefferson, was to extract resources. Jefferson commissioned the Lewis and Clark Expedition or Corps of Discovery (1803–1806) to map and describe the land west of the Mississippi and find a waterway to the Pacific Ocean. The West served as a passage for global trade, fueled by furs that were in great demand in Asia and India.

In 1811, John Jacob Astor commissioned Wilson Price Hunt to lead a fur-finding expedition. On their way up the Missouri at the mouth of the Niobrara River, the party met three men: John Hoback, a mountain man and trapper, and his two companions, Edward Robinson and Jacob Reznor.

They had come west from farms in Kentucky in 1810 and had canoed up the Missouri River with Andrew Henry and helped him build Henry's Fort. Now disillusioned, they intended to return home. Warned by Hoback against taking the northern route along the Missouri River where the Blackfeet were a threat, Hunt convinced the trapper and his companions to change their plans. He asked them to lead his party overland through present-day Wyoming over the route they had just traveled. Following Indian trails, Hoback led Hunt's party back across the Big Horn Mountains and down the Big Horn River to the place where it turns west and becomes the Wind River.

Then they took a route, later called Union Pass, that took them north of the Wind River Range and down the Green River to the point where it turned east. By then it was September. Just east of The Rim of the Hoback Basin, the Shoshones were camped communally, killing mountain bison and drying the meat for their yearly journey south. Hunt bartered with them to restock his company's meat supply.

Then the party continued west, following the river through what are now the Hoback Basin and the town of Bondurant and through the steep and challenging Hoback Canyon to its confluence with the Snake River. Other than a few trappers who may have visited the Hoback Basin in search of beaver, Hunt's party included the first documented white explorers to move through this region. Marie Dorian, a mixed-blood woman and wife of one of the interpreters, is remembered for her valor.

Hunt still envisioned a waterway to the Pacific Ocean. When his group reached the Snake River, against the advice of Indian guides and trappers, he made an unsuccessful attempt to continue the journey by water. After loss of lives and provisions, he consented to follow John Hoback over what is now Teton Pass into present-day Idaho.

At this point, John Hoback and his friends abandoned their plans to return to Kentucky and went back to trapping. Hunt's party dispersed and, alone or in small groups, continued the arduous overland journey to Astoria, Oregon. After years of trapping and surviving the elements, Hoback and his companions were killed by Indians who were retaliating for the death of one of their braves, shot by the soldiers for stealing. Thus, John Hoback, a trapper and guide who had played his part in inaugurating the fur-trade era in the West, met an ignominious end. No marker identifies his grave, so it is fitting that the place names of the Hoback honor him.

Hoback represents many young men like him who lost their lives as the United States expanded westward. Although mountain men have sometimes been characterized as misanthropic, brutish, anarchic, and antisocial, they led difficult lives, facing "harsh weather, wearying distances, the threat of starvation, and oppressive solitude."[3] They chose a life in the wild that—although survival oriented—was also self-contained and fulfilling, as portrayed by Osborne Russell in his journals.[4] Seeking a means of earning a living, they were not unlike present oil and gas workers who come to this country to find employment.

Indian hostilities were a constant threat during the fur-trading days, which is understandable. Through treaty, direct conflict, starvation, and confinement to reservations where they were expected to learn to farm, the original inhabitants of this land were displaced or killed to solve the "Indian problem." The Shoshones, who were not a warring tribe, in an effort to survive, conducted raids on trappers and immigrants to steal their horses. Later they traded these horses, as well as dogs, as food to starving trappers or immigrants caught on the trail by snow and freezing temperatures. The displacement of native people, although not a major theme of this book, is an important aspect of westward expansion.

By the mid-1800s, when beaver had nearly been exterminated, bison were slaughtered ruthlessly to satisfy the eastern appetite for hides and caps as well as to starve Indian people. Fur trade and subsistence hunting also took a heavy toll on wildlife populations as more people moved through and into the Hoback and surrounding country. Companies like the Pacific Fur Company hired hunters to kill wild game to supply meat on their forays. On their own journeys through the region, trappers and immigrants often went hungry since wild game had become scarce. Bighorn sheep, bison, gray wolves, and grizzly bears were eventually extirpated, and the populations of elk, mule deer, and pronghorn, as well as beaver, were severely reduced.

Attitudes toward wildlife and land conservation began to change by the mid-nineteenth century. The first law establishing hunting seasons in Wyoming Territory was passed in 1875 before Wyoming became a state in 1890. With this law, recreational hunting was acknowledged as an intrinsic part of the culture and regulated to reverse the decline of wildlife populations. Hunting persists to this day, providing a livelihood for outfitters and a source of meat for many residents of the Hoback Basin. Hunting outfitters and individuals were among the first to organize to protect the Wyoming Range from oil and gas development.

AFTER THE FUR trade ended around 1850, unrestricted settlement of the land began. The most apt description of this period is "lawless": no federal regulations protected the land occupied by miners and settlers, and the lack of restrictions on land acquisition encouraged speculation and exploitation of resources. The government sold land for a pittance to people who wanted a new beginning as well as to foreigners, like my ancestors, who saw an opportunity to overcome their poverty. Squatters were allowed to buy the federal land they had settled, as well as underground mineral rights. Miners could prospect anywhere on public lands where they could file legitimate claims.

This era was also lawless because some people found it more lucrative to steal from others than to toil on their own homesteads. These rustlers drove off cattle or horses on the open range and claimed them as their own. They could change brands on cattle and horses by burning in new marks and altering the old ones. Rustling continued into the first decades of the twentieth century.

As a child at meals at the big round table with my parents and hired men at our ranch on Hams Fork River in the early 1930s, I recall many tales about rustlers. Especially intriguing was the story of Annie Richey, who was jailed for rustling but died in her cell of poisoning before she was brought to trial. And once when some of our sheep disappeared in our pasture just before shearing, Dad was convinced they had been stolen. An ideal time to steal sheep was right before shearing, when the wool could be cut off, the previous painted brand removed, and the rustler's brand substituted. Earmarks could be "worked over." Dad did not involve the sheriff because he was convinced nothing would be done. But later, when he met the rustler in a bar, Dad invited him into the alley and beat him soundly. My father, a small, tough Italian, had learned to settle his disputes with his fists, much to the dismay of my mother.

THE FORESTED LANDS in what would become Wyoming were considered open range for ranchers who trailed their sheep or cattle into the mountains for summer grazing. Because of unregulated grazing, as well as extraction of minerals and timber, tell-tale signs of damage to the land began to appear. Federal policies attempted to stem environmental degradation and legalize and control settlement. The Preemption Act of 1841 was an effort to discourage unlawful settlement.

The Homestead Act of 1862 further encouraged lawful settlement by allowing settlers to acquire 160 acres if they could "prove up" on a claim by cultivating the land and building structures within five years. The 160 acres was based on how much land a farmer in the East would need with ample rainfall. In the arid west, and especially in higher elevations like the Hoback Basin, 160 acres were too little for ranching. The result was consolidation of homesteads into large ranches or people filing speculatively on homesteads for later sale.[5]

Settlement of the Hoback Basin began as homesteaders moved in. Long before arrival of the first known explorers, however, the Shoshones inhabited the area seasonally to hunt game. The Mountain Shoshones were horseless and moved up and down the Greater Yellowstone region, including the Gros Ventre and Wind River Ranges.

After settlement, Indians had treaty rights to hunt on unoccupied public land, but by the mid-nineteenth century, even remote parts of Wyoming such as the Hoback were being settled. As more Euro-Americans moved into the area, conflicts with Native people intensified. In 1895, a fracas over hunting rights, which resulted in the death of two Indians, took place near what is now called Battle Mountain, near the mouth of Granite Creek in Hoback Canyon. The Indians' unrestricted hunting rights had begun to annoy white settlers in Jackson Hole who earned their living by guiding hunting parties. One of the most accurate accounts, researched by University of Utah historian Brigham Madsen, describes the so-called battle.

On July 15, 1895, a group of twenty-seven armed men captured and disarmed a hunting party of nine Indians traveling with their families. After marching the group for a whole day, the men began to load cartridges into the empty chambers of their guns, and, thinking they were to be killed, the Indians made a break for the

FIGURE 9. Near Battle Mountain *(in the foreground)* on the north bank of the Hoback River, a fracas over hunting rights resulted in the death of two Indians in 1895. Photo: Susan Marsh.

woods. During the melee, one Indian was killed and another seriously wounded. Two children were lost; one was never found.[6]

The Office of Indian Affairs then forged an agreement with Wyoming's Governor Richards to bring a test case on hunting rights before the courts. Judge John A. Riner affirmed the rights of the Shoshone and Bannock Indians to hunt on unoccupied public land, but the case was immediately appealed to the U.S. Supreme Court and ultimately reversed on May 25, 1896, in *Ward v. Race Horse,* which took away Indian rights to hunt.

The resolution of the dispute repeated the injustices to Native Americans, whose rights to land as well as hunting were repeatedly usurped.

This skirmish foreshadowed the contemporary controversy, when major actors shifted from Native Americans to outfitters and recreational hunters, who joined environmentalists in opposing energy development in the heart of the Wyoming Range.

DURING THE PRESIDENCY of Theodore Roosevelt, the Forest Transfer Act of 1905 established the USFS. With the advice and planning of Chief Forester Gifford Pinchot, 148 million acres of new national forests were reserved. Although Pinchot's ideas were utilitarian and favored timber harvesting, he left the national forests with this directive: "Where conflicting interests must be

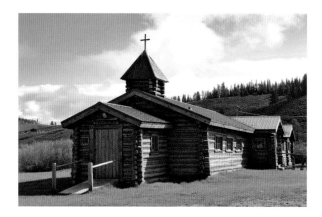

FIGURE 10. St. Hubert the Hunter Church, founded in 1941, is now listed in the National Register of Historic Places. Photo: Susan Marsh.

FIGURE 11. Bondurant's public library was built adjacent to St. Hubert the Hunter Church in 1943. The two historic structures still serve as the main community gathering places for the citizens of Bondurant. Photo: Susan Marsh.

reconciled, the question shall always be answered from the standpoint of the greatest good of the greatest number in the long run."[7]

The USFS brought forest rangers to manage the forests and oversee grazing permits. One of the first forest rangers hired in the Hoback Basin was Benjamin Franklin Bondurant. He added ranger duties to the many other endeavors he and his wife, Ella, had undertaken in the basin. They had come by wagon at the turn of the nineteenth century. Although this was not their planned destination, they decided to stay. They opened

a guesthouse, one of the first resort-based outfitting businesses in Wyoming. Tourists got their meals in the main ranch house, and tents and several cabins were later added to house visiting dudes. On June 30, 1903, the couple opened the first U.S. Post Office in Bondurant.

As settlement increased in the Hoback Basin during the early twentieth century, a road, connecting it to Pinedale on one side and Jackson Hole on the other, became essential. The Oregon and Lander Trails, along with a whole series of other trails that led to areas that would become the states of New Mexico, Utah, Nevada, Idaho, California, Oregon, and Washington, avoided passing through treacherous Hoback Canyon, which was too rugged for wagons. Instead, the network of trails crossed the Wyoming Range south of present-day La Barge, where the names of pioneers were inscribed on a sandstone outcrop called Names Hill. A wagon road from the Rim to Bondurant was in use by 1907, but it wasn't until five years later that it continued through the canyon to Jackson Hole. In 1916, the first two automobiles were driven from Jackson to Pinedale along the Hoback road.

Around the same time, the USFS became more of a presence in the Hoback Basin. A ranger station was established, and some forest roads and trails were constructed in the early years, primarily for fighting fires and providing access to logs for housing.

In an effort to ease the economic hardships of the Great Depression, President Franklin D. Roosevelt created the Civilian Conservation Corps (CCC) in 1933, a New Deal work-relief program that focused on preserving natural resources. Unemployed men and a small number of women between the ages of eighteen and twenty-five built firebreaks, national-forest lookouts, bridges, campgrounds, trails, and museums in national forests and parks. They received room and board and thirty dollars a month for their

FIGURE 12. Civilian Conservation Corps Camp F-6 at the mouth of Cliff Creek in 1935. The men housed here constructed the pool and bathhouse at Granite Hot Springs, Hoback Campground and Guard Station, and the fire lookout on Monument Ridge, all of which remain today. Photo courtesy of the BTNF historical photo collection.

FIGURE 13. The Hoback Guard Station, completed in 1935. The structure still houses seasonal crews and can be rented by the public when the USFS is not using it. Photo: Susan Marsh.

hard work, twenty-five of which had to be sent home. The men from CCC Camp F-6 constructed the pool and bathhouse at Granite Hot Springs, Hoback Campground, and Hoback Guard Station. (The latter, completed in 1935, is eligible for the National Register of Historic Places.) They also built the fire lookout on Monument Ridge.

It, too, is eligible for the National Register of Historic Places.

In the subsequent decades, the pace of growth in the Hoback Basin has been moderate, and the character of the land has changed relatively little. About fifty homesteaders first filed land claims in the basin. Over the years, larger ranches purchased

FIGURE 14. Monument Ridge lookout with the Gros Ventre Range and Hoback Basin in the distance. Photo: Susan Marsh.

many of the homesteads to form the seven ranches that exist today. The Little Jenny and Jackson Fork Ranches are the largest. The Campbell family occupies the only ranch that contains land originally homesteaded by its ancestors. As is the case with all ranches adjacent to the BTNF, the owners run their cattle on forest allotments in the summer. The ranchers cooperatively manage the summer grazing of their cattle through associations like the Hoback Stock Association. It hires Tom Filkins to be its range rider. Each summer, with several other cowboys, he moves and distributes the cattle, preventing overgrazing within the forest.

According to the 2010 U.S. Census, the post office for the 82922 zip code, including Bondurant and the surrounding area, delivers mail to 257 households. Several housing developments have grown up on old homesteads in the foothills in the upper and lower Hoback and on Jack Creek near the Gros Ventres. Hoback Ranches is a large development on The Rim of the Wyoming Range, overlooking the Hoback Basin. My cabin is part of a small development in the lower Hoback three miles from the town of Bondurant that was created in the 1960s on an old homestead. The cabin, built in 1990, sits in a meadow in the shadow of Clark Butte with open vistas of the Gros Ventre and Hoback Ranges. With my husband, Paul, and after he died in 1996, I have lived in the cabin half of each year, and one year I stayed through the winter, which was one of the most memorable experiences of my life. The Hoback Basin in winter is beautiful beyond belief, but as an older woman living alone, I found it quite challenging.[8]

FIGURE 15. Tom Filkins, range rider for the Hoback Stock Association, delivering salt to cattle on their summer range. Photo: Susan Marsh.

FIGURE 16. Putting up hay on the Little Jenny Ranch, one of the largest cattle ranches in Hoback Basin. Photo: Susan Marsh.

Typical of those who live in a state like Wyoming, the people in the Hoback Basin are industrious and self-sufficient and represent a heterogeneous array of skilled and unskilled workers, professionals, and retirees. Many of the permanent residents drive to work each day in Jackson or Pinedale. The small population, the people's independence, and a handful of public gathering places interact to unify the residents.

The town of Bondurant is unincorporated and has no council to handle affairs. The Bondurant Community Club is primarily a social and civic organization that plans events, such as the summer barbeque and the yearly heritage sale, and brings the residents together several times a year to celebrate the seasons. It is also a socially conscious organization that cares for those in need. The Hoback Fire Department not only manages to put out fires throughout the basin but, with trained personnel, also responds to injuries, automobile accidents, or residents in distress.

THE HOBACK IS known for its proximity to vast areas of backcountry and is the gateway into the Wyoming Range and Gros Ventre Wilderness, which offer boundless possibilities for recreation as well as critical habitat for wildlife and a source of clean, abundant water for downstream use. While it may be easy for those of us who live here to take the backcountry for granted, when seen in

FIGURE 17. Flo Shepard's cabin in Hoback Basin, where she spent one winter alone. Photo: Florence Shepard.

a national context, wildlands—those that are not settled or cultivated—are becoming increasingly rare. Even within the national forest system, which contains more backcountry than the national parks combined, many forests can offer their visitors only a narrow choice between classified wilderness (much of it overcrowded) and roaded, developed areas; there isn't much backcountry left.

The BTNF, and the Wyoming Range in particular, offers backcountry in abundance. In addition to wilderness and backcountry, the Hoback Basin has a number of lightly traveled forest roads that offer camping. People value the chance to get off by themselves, and the places they frequent are very special to them. For both backcountry travelers and users of the roads and campsites, the opportunity to see wildlife and enjoy scenic settings is very important. The wildlands surrounding the Hoback Basin include the Gros Ventre Wilderness and adjacent Shoal Creek Wilderness Study Area, both designated by Congress in 1984. Together they comprise 317,000 acres. In addition, several smaller backcountry locales designated by the USFS as "areas with wilderness potential" include Muddy Creek, Noble Basin, Raspberry Ridge, and Monument Ridge, adding another 48,500 acres.

To the south, the Hoback Range is part of the 315,000-acre Grayback Roadless Area in the northern part of the Wyoming Range with miles

The national forest surrounding the Hoback Basin includes the Gros Ventre Wilderness and adjacent Shoal Creek Wilderness Study Area, both designated by Congress in 1984, as well as hundreds of thousands of acres of roadless backcountry in the northern Wyoming Range.

Rust-red outcrops near West Dell Falls in the Gros Ventre Wilderness. Photo: Susan Marsh.

The Hoback Range from the Shoal Falls Trail in the Shoal Creek Wilderness Study Area. Photo: Susan Marsh.

Lander Peak on the east side of the Wyoming Range. Many undeveloped energy leases are nearby. Photo: Susan Marsh.

of trails leading deeply into some of Wyoming's most spectacular wild country. The Wyoming Range National Recreation Trail, created primarily for hiking and backpacking, runs for more than seventy miles. Though the range is vast, many places are reasonably accessible, with peaks and alpine lakes lying within a few miles of a gravel-surfaced forest road.

The Wyoming Range, though it extends for nearly a hundred miles south of the Hoback Basin, is a major part of this story. More than a series of attractions, the appeal of the Wyoming Range is its singularity as a place. The "feel" of it is different from that of mountains to the north and east; each person who experiences the range has a unique set of reasons why it is special.

FIGURE 18. Sunrise lights the eastern front of the Wyoming Range. The white outcrop divides Middle Piney Canyon from Straight Creek Canyon. Photo courtesy of Rita Donham, Wyoming Aero Photo.

Considered a minor range by mountaineers and part of our backdoor wilderness and place of livelihood by many local residents, the Wyoming Range has been overlooked by the public. Since the mid-1990s, perceptions have changed as controversy over energy development has shone a spotlight on the range. Several guidebooks now attract recreationists looking to avoid the crowds in the Tetons and Wind River Range.

The backdrop for controversy was in place as plans developed for exploratory drilling in the Hoback Basin: the independent people who lived there cherished this wild country. The love and lure of the backcountry—acres of pristine mountain habitat, including wilderness, primitive, and roadless areas where nature is still pristine and offers beauty and solace to people wearied by the press of civilization—held them. The inhabitants dwelled within their surroundings, philosophically and literally, and had become, in author Wes Jackson's words, native to a place.[9]

3

From Timber to Gas Wells
(1946–1990)

....

SUNRISE IN NEVADA, THE SPRING OF 1946. After a sleepless night on a train headed east, I rose from my seat and worked my way back through the cars of sleeping passengers to the caboose and stepped out on the platform. A rain shower had just moved through the countryside, and the fragrance of wet sagebrush brought tears to my eyes. I was returning from college in California and would soon be home on the sheep ranch in Wyoming. The previous summer had not been a good one: two bombs dropped by our forces had killed a quarter of a million Japanese civilians. Their slaughter shattered my heartfelt patriotism, nurtured through the years of my youth and throughout World War II.

I hoped this would be a better summer, but recent news from home had left me apprehensive. I'd be returning to a postwar landscape with many changes. Much to my dismay, the wild horses on public lands—the sagebrush steppe surrounding the ranch that we called the Desert—were being rounded up and sold for dog food. And the coyotes would no longer leap from their cover as we galloped by on our horses. These ubiquitous carnivores were being poisoned out of existence, and with them other carrion feeders, such as golden eagles. With enemies of war defeated, it was as if the West had turned on wild animals to vent its anger.

The sheep ranch ran along the banks of the Hams Fork River, whose waters flowed from the Wyoming Range to the north. Homesteaders along the river in the late nineteenth century had grubbed the sagebrush and planted the meadows with English hay (a combination of hearty grasses—timothy, redtop, and smooth brome—along with red clover). Settlers followed this practice of planting hay fields as they moved westward through virgin forests and grasslands to the sagebrush steppe of Wyoming and beyond to the Pacific. When mature, the hay was cut and stored for winter fodder for livestock.

Homesteaders who proved up on the acres that later became our ranch were allowed to cut timber in the forests of the Wyoming Range about fifty miles away. They built a house and

FIGURE 19. A ranch truck loaded with hay, circa 1945. Photo: Florence Shepard.

barn of harvested logs. Other buildings were constructed from sandstone quarried from the surrounding hills. At almost 7,000 feet, the ranch and river were surrounded by sagebrush stretching for miles across southwestern Wyoming. Along the willow-lined banks of the Hams Fork River near the log house, a grove of huge cottonwoods and a small "orchard" of hawberry were the only trees.

Many changes had taken place on the ranch since the end of World War II. With wartime rationing and shortages over, Wyoming experienced a wave of industrialization and accompanying sociological and economic changes. Housing was constructed for returning veterans and their growing families. New cars were appearing, many of them Studebakers, sold at my father's garage in Kemmerer, twelve miles west of our ranch, where he had started a dealership after the war.

Riding the wave of postwar prosperity, Dad began to mechanize the ranch. He bought a war-surplus Jeep, so we no longer rode horses to check on livestock and fences. Uncle Jim, my mother's brother, designed a hay pusher out of our old '28 Cadillac with the wheelbase reversed so that it maneuvered easily to pick up the raked rows at haying time. Tractors replaced the horses for raking and mowing, and a big Ford truck substituted for the team that pulled the hayrack.

Dad buried a huge gas tank in the yard and installed a pump. A distributor from Kemmerer sent a tanker periodically to replenish the supply so there was always available fuel for the machines. Our ranch was a microcosm of nationwide industrialization, and concomitantly a part of the increasing demand for fuel that spurred energy exploration and development. The local coal company sold out to a large mining corporation, which expanded the mines into a strip development that fed newly constructed regional power plants, including one on the outskirts of

FIGURE 20. Sheep camp on the winter range, circa 1939.
Photographer unknown, Florence Shepard photo collection.

Kemmerer. Seismograph crews crisscrossed the sagebrush steppe, exploring for gas and oil on our land and adjoining federal rangeland. Always the optimistic entrepreneur, Dad welcomed exploration and contracts with energy companies. After all, small up-front payments could mushroom into huge royalties if oil was discovered.

When Dad bought the Hams Fork ranch in the late 1920s, sheep ranchers followed the practice of homesteaders before them, grazing their sheep on the open range near their property that was owned by the U. S. government. In 1934, Congress passed the Taylor Grazing Act, establishing the U. S. Grazing Service, which made this common practice legal. However, without government control of numbers of livestock, overgrazing and soil erosion became serious problems exacerbated by a lengthy and persistent drought. Finally in 1946, Congress created the BLM with jurisdiction over the sagebrush/bunchgrass steppe, which

dominated most of Wyoming, except for the forests at higher elevations.

The BLM seemed to mesh perfectly with Dad's plan to improve production on the ranch and make it more self-contained. The agency gave him permission to fence 10,000 acres of the Carter lease adjoining the ranch. As I recall, the BLM also provided poles and barbed wire for fencing and contracted with him to build a reservoir at Coyote Springs on Carter-lease BLM land.

The BLM sagebrush/bunchgrass rangeland near the ranch provided perfect winter grazing for sheep. Wyoming winds cleared the snow from the dried grasses and forbs that sheep feed on and piled it in drifts beside the sagebrush. Both sheep and horses can eat snow as their source of water, whereas cattle have to winter near running water.

To add to his efforts to utilize public lands for his sheep-ranching enterprise, Dad had been looking for summer grazing rights in the BTNF

FIGURE 21. View across La Barge Creek toward Mount Graham from the Tri Basin Divide, where Florence's family summered its band of sheep. Photo: Susan Marsh.

to the north. Until that time, he had been leasing summer grazing land on the Bear River. The portion of the BTNF along La Barge Creek in the southern Wyoming Range was close enough for sheep to be trailed from our ranch in early summer and back again in the fall, where they wintered on BLM rangeland adjoining the ranch. However, forest permits could not be bought outright; they could only be acquired by buying land adjacent to the national forests and applying for a grazing permit.

When a rancher in the La Barge area with BTNF grazing permits decided to sell his lambing ground with grazing rights, Dad bought the land.

With the land came underground mineral rights. After recovering from the Great Depression, Dad was short on cash and already had suitable lambing grounds near the ranch, so he sold the newly purchased land but retained the forest permits, as well as half of the mineral rights. This sort of speculation had been common since the expansion era in the United States, which had encouraged private settlement of public lands.[1]

The forest allotments on La Barge Creek and Greys River in the Wyoming Range were an excellent addition to our small ranching enterprise and a source of enjoyment for Dad, who found them similar to his homeland in the alpine Austrian

Tyrol. Our family looked forward to camping on La Barge Creek each summer, and at other times, when Dad had to deliver supplies to the sheep-herders in the mountains, I eagerly accompanied him. On these journeys, as we drove up the La Barge Road, Dad predicted that someday the area would become a large oil field.

Dad based his conclusion on historic facts. Oil seeps had been found in the region in 1907. The first producing oil well in the Rocky Mountains was drilled in 1924, and a small enterprise still operated in a tiny Wyoming settlement called Tulsa. In the winter of 1938, a gas well blew out in that area; it took two months to bring it under control, indicating vast underground reserves. Intermittent wildcat drilling continued, but any discoveries had limited commercial potential.

The California Oil Company, later called Chevron, drilled for oil on the Pinedale Anticline in 1939. The company did not find oil, but there was much natural gas, for which there was no demand at the time. Company officials were convinced that there was oil in the area, but it was much deeper and locked in sandstone, and they had no successful technology to extract it. The El Paso Gas Company purchased rights to this well, and during the 1940s and '50s drilled seven new wells, also without commercial success. Together with the Meridian Oil Company, they continued to find natural gas in the area. El Paso Gas built a refining facility in Opal, the small railroad stop where I had attended a one-room school. Meridian and El Paso built several pipelines, but none of the drilling sites proved exceptional, so production was low.

SINCE THE EARLY 1930s—when droughts over most of the land west of the Mississippi created the dust bowl—naturalists, foresters, and game managers had been greatly concerned about steadily harvesting timber in western forests and overgrazing rangeland. Mining was unrestricted, and there were no laws to protect the flora, fauna,

and soil as mineral and energy development proceeded. The regional ranching culture, whose origins lay in the open and unrestricted rangeland of homesteading days, objected to proposed regulations to control grazing on BLM lands, although USFS grazing had been regulated for more than twenty years.

As the degradation of rangelands and forests continued during the late nineteenth and early twentieth centuries, an ethos to preserve wild, untrammeled nature was growing among naturalists and game managers. But long before a general awareness of the environment took hold among Americans, at least one local rancher believed wildlife and wildland were worth protecting. Carroll Noble, whose name lives on in Noble Basin east of the upper Hoback River (the very place where the controversy over PXP drilling of natural gas wells arose), championed preserving the Wind River Range during the 1930s. He suffered a great deal of castigation from his fellow ranchers but continued to work to preserve natural resources in the local area and the state. With Tom Bell, journalist and editor of *High Country News,* Noble cofounded the Wyoming Outdoor Council (WOC), and he also took a leadership role in the National Wildlife Federation. His family still ranches in the Cora area, where his parents homesteaded in 1897.[2]

In 1935, Bob Marshall, head of recreation management for the USFS in Montana, was a key figure in bringing wilderness preservation into the public eye. He provided leadership and initial funding for the Wilderness Society (TWS), which he and a group of naturalists and scientists had founded. Among them were Olaus Murie, Aldo Leopold, Sigurd Olson, Celia Hunter, and Howard Zahniser. The movement was well established at the time of Marshall's untimely death in 1939 and carried his legacy forward.

Starting in the 1940s, committed naturalists and scientists met regularly with the Muries, who

FIGURE 22. Erosion gully on the north slope of Sheep Pass, where up to 300,000 sheep traveled twice annually between 1895 and 1905. More than five feet of soil turned to dust under those hooves, and the land is still slowly recovering. Photo: Susan Marsh.

had moved to Moose in Jackson Hole, Wyoming. Brothers Olaus and Adolph Murie had conducted studies for the U.S. Biological Survey and National Park Service in Alaska on caribou and wolves. By the time they and their wives, Mardy and Louise, had settled in Jackson Hole, they were well-known advocates for conservation.

In 1945, they bought the STS Dude Ranch, where they carried on their conservation work. Along with cabins for the Murie households, several small sleeping cabins provided housing and a meeting place for progressive conservationists. Murie became president of TWS in 1950, and it was at the Murie Ranch that the group developed the parameters for national protection of wilderness. When Olaus died in 1963, his wife, Mardy, took over as a national figure advocating wilderness preservation. The ranch is presently a historic site and houses the Murie Center, an organization that continues to emphasize the value of wilderness and develop a new generation of conservationists.

Aldo Leopold's *A Sand County Almanac,* published in 1949 shortly after he had died of a heart attack while fighting a neighbor's grass fire, made a significant contribution to the growth of a conservation ethic. The book begins with these words: "There are some who can live without wild things, and some who cannot. These essays are the delights and dilemmas of one who cannot."[3] It was a book for the time and spoke to the hearts and minds of people who had become conscious of the beauty and value of undomesticated wild nature. Along with Leopold's other books, *A Sand County Almanac* became required reading in university courses for future wildlife biologists and foresters. Leopold had planted the seed of environmentalism in the loam of conservation ethics, and it began to grow.

One of the first places where it took hold was Jackson, Wyoming. The nation had become hungry for fuel, and Wyoming was about to

FIGURE 23. *Left to right:* Aldo Leopold and Olaus Murie at an annual meeting of the council of the Wilderness Society at Old Rag Mountain, Virginia, in 1946. Photo: National Conservation Training Center Museum archives, United States Fish and Wildlife Service, courtesy of the Murie Center.

become a major producer. Energy development to the east and west of the Hoback Basin had begun to encroach upon wild things that many locals could not live without. In Jackson Hole, a diverse group of scientists and naturalists, federal and local officials, and business owners and citizens joined to address potential environmental consequences of oil and gas drilling in the area. They contacted Secretary of the Interior Julius Albert Krug, appointed in 1946 by President Truman. Krug had been the chief engineer for the Tennessee Valley Authority and held subsequent government positions overseeing power development. His experience on the ground in the aftermath of energy production gave him special insight into its consequences.

Krug became involved in the Jackson Hole issue as citizens and federal land managers in the Department of the Interior showed increasing concern about mineral leases near Grand Teton National Park and the National Elk Refuge, operated by the United States Fish and Wildlife Service (USFWS). They pointed out that energy exploration anywhere near Grand Teton National Park threatened the primary values of the region for recreation and nature appreciation. Furthermore, they asserted, it would disrupt the migration of thousands of elk that winter on the National Elk Refuge and in the surrounding mountains.

The proposals presented by the local groups suggested that Secretary Krug restrict all leasing north of the tenth standard parallel, which runs just south of the town of Jackson. After a visit to the area and a year of contemplation, Krug issued a memorandum in 1947 to protect the Jackson Hole area. Much to the consternation of the conservationists, he drew the line beyond which no energy leasing could take place north of the eleventh standard parallel. The park had not yet expanded, so some land within what is now Grand Teton National Park was subject to energy leasing and development, in addition to USFS land.

Krug had not abandoned the national forest south of the eleventh parallel; he formulated provisions that applied to that area as well. During the PXP debate decades in the future, Krug Memorandum stipulations played a major part in stopping natural gas drilling in the Wyoming Range.

The Krug Memorandum and the stipulations that became part of the BTNF forest plan require the following from companies and the USFS:

- To drill wells on leased national forest lands only if they do not harm the surrounding environment;
- After drilling, to remove all facilities except those essential for the continuing operation of the well;
- To keep at an absolute minimum all roads and to place them so that they don't cause damage to the environment;
- To protect the scenic value of roadsides, waterways, and recreation areas;
- To protect wildlife near the leased land and on adjacent forest land; and
- To protect the quality of municipal water.[4]

The Krug Memorandum was soon tested as the energy industry, already interested in parts of the Jackson Hole area and Hoback Basin, began filing applications with the BLM to drill in the Green River Basin. In the 1950s, development expanded rapidly as areas near Jackson Hole (Moccasin Basin, Little Granite Creek, and Cache Creek) were identified as having potential energy resources.

At the time Secretary Krug issued his memorandum for the Jackson Hole area, energy exploration was already under way seventy miles to the east in the Green River Basin south of Pinedale. In the future, large gas operations would develop on the Jonah Field and Pinedale Anticline, and the Moxa Arch and La Barge Platform on the eastern slopes of the Wyoming Range.

The lambing ground my father had purchased to secure grazing permits in the BTNF was part of the La Barge Platform. During the late 1950s, the mineral rights that he retained began paying off. By that time, my father was in ill health, and my parents had sold the ranch. They used one of their first sizeable royalty checks to take an extended journey to Europe. They bought a little red Fiat, visited relatives in Italy, and traveled elsewhere in Europe to satisfy my father's doubts about the atrocities against the Jews that he felt had been propaganda to draw the United States into the war. Unfortunately, he learned that the extermination camps had been a reality, and to his dying day, he could not reconcile how a people who had given him sustenance as a child could have committed such crimes. Motherless, from a destitute Tyrolean family in the small village of Tret, he had been sent to San Felice, a German-speaking village a short distance across the Austrian border, where he was employed and

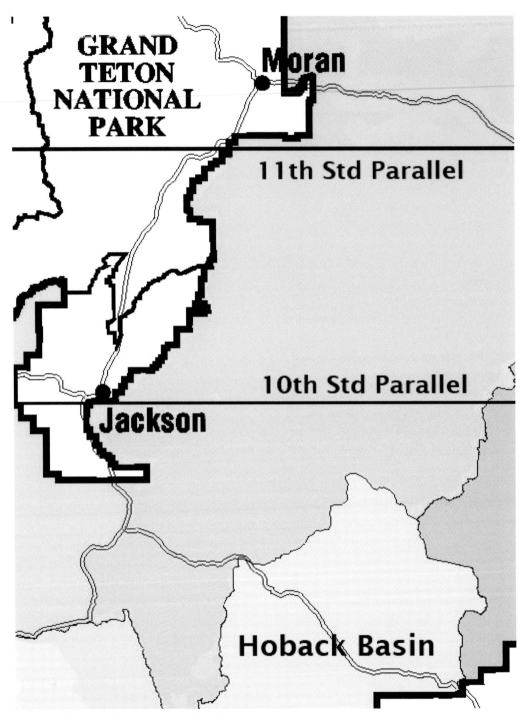

MAP 4. The area in the BTNF covered by the Krug Memorandum, written by Secretary of the Interior Julius Albert Krug in 1947. This memorandum is the basis for energy-development stipulations in the 1990 forest plan. Map courtesy of the USFS.

given board and room. As he recalled, it was the only time during his childhood when he had not gone hungry. By the end of his European travels, he had accepted the realities of the Holocaust.

When the search for oil began, many ranchers in the Green River Basin signed agreements for energy exploration on their land much as my father had, with the same hope of profit if oil or gas was discovered on their property. The sight and sound of an oil pump or gas well was something they assumed they could cope with.

IN THE YEARS immediately following World War II, concerns about environmental effects of energy production were not primary newsmakers. Led by Wyoming's Olaus and Mardy Murie, citizen activists began pushing to protect North Slope wildlife ranges in Alaska during the 1950s. Meanwhile, legislation and policy conveyed large tracts of western public lands to the military and the Atomic Energy Commission. Hard-rock mining of strategic minerals like uranium proliferated during the Cold War. At the same time, conservation was operating as parcels of national forest and BLM land were protected from mineral exploration to preserve their scenic and recreational value.

Citizens at that time were particularly concerned about accelerated harvesting of forests, primarily by clear-cutting. At the beginning of World War II, less than 2 percent of the nation's wood was derived from USFS timber sales.[5] This changed when the newly affluent postwar nation demanded more commodities. Rapid depletion of old-growth timber on private lands resulted in increased invasion of national forests. During the 1950s, annual USFS timber harvests soared from about three billion to almost nine billion board feet.[6]

By the end of the 1950s, the rate of trees harvested from national forests had accelerated so much that people were agreeing with Bob Marshall, who had observed decades before that "wilderness is melting away like some last snowbank on some south-facing mountainside during a hot afternoon in June. It is disappearing while most of those who care more for it than anything else in the world are trying desperately to rally and save it."[7]

THE 1960s SAW the passage of national legislation to address growing public concern that the USFS was favoring the timber industry at the expense of other forest values. The first was the Multiple-Use Sustained-Yield Act of 1960, which guided government agencies toward a "harmonious and coordinated management of the various resources . . . without impairment of the productivity of the land, with consideration being given to the relative values of the various resources, and not necessarily the combination of uses that will give the greatest dollar return or the greatest unit output."[8] This set the stage for considering not only commodity production but also preservation of wildland. Changes in the way public lands were used followed, including setting aside campgrounds and ski areas for recreation, protecting wildlife habitat, and designating historic, geologic, and botanical sites. The eastern part of the North Slope of Alaska was designated a federal protected area eight years before the Prudhoe Bay oil field was discovered.

As a biology teacher in Kemmerer, Wyoming, and the mother of four young children, I was preoccupied with getting through each day and isolated from national environmental issues. One summer—needing teacher-recertification credit—I decided to attend the Audubon Society's Camp of the West near Dubois, Wyoming. In the rich habitat of the foothills of the Wind River Range, scientists and naturalists taught courses that focused on geology, ecology, flora, and fauna.

I was as impressed by the participants as I was by the teachers and the landscape. I watched in amazement when all instruction ceased as a group stood for what seemed like an hour seriously discussing whether a little brown bird in the willows had an eye ring. As a child and even through college, I had lived close to nature. But the love and respect for nature that my parents felt were often overshadowed by the pragmatic need to scrape a living from the Wyoming steppes. The people at the camp had a serious relationship with this little bird, and they thought it was important to know precisely who it was. Wanting to conform, I joined the group and discovered the joys of bird-watching. It remains to this day one of the things I love best.

For the first time, I read Leopold's *A Sand County Almanac,* one of the most influential books in my life. It—as well as two weeks of inspirational instruction and interaction with nature lovers from throughout the country—changed my life. I felt ashamed for not questioning the environmental destruction that I witnessed around me each day. The conservation ethic voiced by the instructors and Leopold redirected my teaching and refocused my heart and mind on understanding and protecting the natural world.

As my sentiments about the environment changed so did those of the nation as a whole. The 1960s ushered in a period of landmark national legislation to solve ecological problems. On September 3, 1964, President Lyndon Johnson signed the Wilderness Act, which established 9.1 million acres of primitive land as the world's first national wilderness-preservation system. The act's definition of wilderness guided agencies and citizens in selecting additional areas: "A wilderness, in contrast with those areas where man and his own works dominate the landscape, is hereby recognized as an area where the earth and community of life are untrammeled by man, where man himself is a visitor who does not remain."[9] The act was largely drafted by Howard Zahniser, part of a group of naturalists and scientists who had been holding conversations about preserving wild places in the United States.

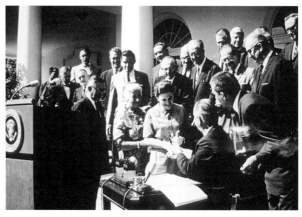

FIGURE 24. *Left to right:* Olaus Murie, Howard Zahniser, and Irving Clark Sr. at a Wilderness Society meeting on the Murie Ranch, circa 1956. Photo courtesy of the Murie Center.

FIGURE 25. President Johnson signs the Wilderness Act into law as Mardy Murie and Alice Zahniser *(left to right, center of photo)* look on. Photo: National Conservation Training Center Museum archives, United States Fish and Wildlife Service, courtesy of the Murie Center.

The Wilderness Act of 1964 introduced a new concept into the conservation lexicon. Special public lands managed by the government were to be held in primal condition for posterity. Rather than promoting more settlement, as had been the case in the past, it prompted a series of policies to protect public lands from population and economic growth. Virgin forests were now worth more than the value of their timber. These forests were recognized as assets for wildlife, watersheds, and recreation.

The Eighty-Ninth Congress (1965–1966), under President Johnson, went on to pass fifty-one conservation measures to address leading environmental issues: water pollution, air pollution, the acquisition and designation of land for public recreation, and the accelerating conversion of farms and forests into urban and suburban areas. In 1968, the Ninetieth Congress created two national parks; three national recreation areas; four wildernesses; a wild, scenic, and recreational river system; and a national trail system— an outstanding contribution to conservation.

The grassroots wilderness movement has grown since the passage of the Wilderness Act partly due to the national activism of organizations like TWS, the Sierra Club, and the Friends of the Earth with their concentration on prime wilderness areas in Alaska and the lower forty-eight states. The idea of wilderness caught on, and state advocacy groups began forming to deal directly with identified areas. The issue of wilderness also became politically charged since new areas had to be designated by members of Congress.

AFTER RETURNING FROM the Camp of the West, I followed through with my commitment to change my biology curriculum. Out of an overgrazed bull pasture near the school, I created an environment where biology students could study their surroundings during the year. With the help of the school board, which bought the property and built boardwalks and fences, I created the exemplary Kemmerer Outdoor Laboratory (KOLAB).

As I grew more ecologically aware, I became more concerned about the environmental problems in southwestern Wyoming caused by coal, oil, and gas development. One day, when I told a school-board member I was worried about the smoke from a new electric power plant on the

outskirts of town, he replied that the smoke was fine with him because it represented more tax dollars.

Disillusioned by the lack of local environmental concern as well as my marriage, I left both my husband and biology teaching in 1969 and moved to Salt Lake City with three of my children (my oldest daughter had married). There I completed a PhD in education and ecology and was appointed an assistant professor in what was then the Department of Educational Studies at the University of Utah. I developed a field course in environmental education for prospective teachers and seminars on environmental issues for teachers pursuing advanced degrees.

At the same time, I continued to work with the Kemmerer School District. A small grant I had received for developing KOLAB included an elementary curriculum component. It provided materials and instruction for elementary teachers to use KOLAB to develop outdoor learning experiences for their pupils. Each summer I taught ecology at the Audubon Camp of the West, where I arranged for scholarships for Kemmerer elementary teachers and students and teachers from the University of Utah. I feel proud and pleased that—while new schools have been built and old schools expanded, KOLAB has remained fenced and protected for fifty years, a beautiful outdoor laboratory of sagebrush steppe for K–12 teachers and pupils in the area.

THE 1970S WERE exciting times for me; I involved students and teachers in pressing regional and national environmental issues. President Richard Nixon encouraged new laws that protected natural resources and the environment. On January 1, 1970, he signed the National Environmental Protection Act (NEPA), a law that greatly altered the way proposals for development on public lands would be reviewed and conducted. The law was established "to create and maintain conditions under which man and nature can exist in productive harmony, and fulfill the social, economic, and other requirements of present and future generations of Americans."[10] NEPA required agencies to involve the public in considering environmental effects of actions they proposed and developing alternatives to mitigate potential effects.

In addition to NEPA, President Nixon signed the Clean Air Act of 1970, the 1972 Clean Water Act, and the Endangered Species Act of 1973. These laws established protocol that is still followed for individual, corporate, or government projects on public lands, including the PXP proposal forty years later. Although President Nixon was condemned for his unethical conduct, he should also be remembered for making environmental reform a part of his legacy.

IN 1973, THE Organization of Petroleum Exporting Countries (OPEC) imposed an embargo that changed our nation's focus on both the cost and availability of energy. The U.S. embarked on some remarkable energy-conservation efforts, including the fifty-five-miles-per-hour speed limit and standards for more efficient autos, appliances, and power plants. At the same time, the desire for domestic energy sources spurred construction of nuclear power plants, field exploration, and development of large projects, none more hotly debated than the trans-Alaska pipeline, built between 1974 and 1977. The massive oil reserve in Prudhoe Bay, Alaska, was discovered in 1968, but production waited until the pipeline was completed. Public debates about the environmental effects of oil production in remote wild areas now became important.

During the 1970s and '80s when I lived in Utah, I served on multiple committees with the USFS, the BLM, and the state, including a panel convened by Utah Governor Scott Matheson to review plans for oil-shale development. At that time, the plan was not feasible because of its

detrimental environmental consequences, cost, and demand for water. I joined other activists in national environmental organizations to oppose the Alaska pipeline and supported the Alaska Native Claims Settlement Act and protection of the Arctic National Wildlife Refuge against exploitation. Following the passage of the Wilderness Act, the secretary of agriculture was directed to conduct a study of areas with wilderness potential. During those years, students and I backpacked into qualified places to inventory their attributes and recommend wilderness status.

In 1967, the USFS undertook its first roadless area review and evaluation (RARE I) to identify these areas. In the report, completed in 1972, the agency found that more than 12 million acres within the national forests were eligible for wilderness designation. Soon after that, several courts ruled that the USFS had not sufficiently complied with NEPA regulations nor given adequate consideration to national grasslands or forests in the eastern U.S.

The agency then began its second roadless area review and evaluation (RARE II). Completed in 1979, RARE II increased potential wilderness to 15 million acres and added 10.8 million acres to a further-study category. The courts also challenged RARE II, partly for its bias emphasizing commodity potential over preservation. The state of California filed suit over roadless areas that had been recommended for nonwilderness status, and the Ninth Circuit Court of Appeals agreed that the final RARE II EIS had not complied with NEPA and required additional review. In 1983, planning regulations were revised to require each national forest's plan to include a review of all areas with wilderness potential.

The final roadless area review (dubbed "RARE II ½") for the BTNF was completed in 1983, identifying nearly 1.8 million acres of potential wilderness within that forest alone. Congress had not waited for final USFS recommendations, however. While various versions of the roadless area review worked their way through revisions and legal challenges, the national wilderness-preservation system grew—through individual bills proposed by legislators and signed into law by the president—to 35 million acres.[11]

DURING THE 1970S, while potential additions to wilderness were being considered, timber harvesting and road building in the national forests attracted public attention. Clear-cutting was the preferred method of removing trees at the time, but it often left unsightly bare patches and eroding road cuts, reduced wildlife habitat, and degraded streams. A court case in 1973 directed the Monongahela National Forest to greatly reduce its amount of clear-cutting. A similar scenario was playing out in Montana along the eastern front of the Bitterroot Range. The BTNF was also in the forefront of political battles over clear-cutting, with Wyoming Senator Gale McGee, as chair of the Agriculture, Environmental, and Consumer Protection Appropriations Subcommittee, taking a prominent role in congressional hearings.

The result of the national controversy over forest practices was passage of the 1976 National Forest Management Act (NFMA). This law set limits on the size of clear-cuts and directed each forest to develop a land and resource-management plan. By the early 1980s, national forests throughout the country were hard at work on forest plans, a process that took at least a decade for most of them.

While timber harvesting was taking center stage nationally, western Wyoming was experiencing an energy boom. By 1980, development was increasing in the upper Green River Basin, now for natural gas more than oil. At the time, eighty-three leases for exploration were pending in the potential wilderness areas of the BTNF, although none of the lessees had asked for a permit to begin drilling. The first requests for exploration included leases in Cache Creek, a popular recreation area and municipal water source for the town of Jackson, and Little Granite Creek, a tributary of Granite Creek, part of which was being considered for inclusion in the proposed Gros Ventre Wilderness. The lessees could not have picked higher-profile sites for their initial drilling requests.

Soon after his inauguration in 1981, President Reagan appointed James Watt as secretary of the interior; Watt wanted to open as much public land as possible, including wilderness areas, to energy development. When locals learned about the proposal to drill in Cache Creek in Jackson Hole through an EIS issued by the BTNF, opposition was intense and immediate. A local consortium of lawyers, backed by town and county government and the Jackson Hole Chamber of Commerce, sued the USFS. At a rally in Cache Creek, Mardy Murie spoke about the opposition of Jackson residents to exploratory drilling. "This valley is a special place," she said. "The people here recognize that the greatest gift we can give the American people is keeping this place as it is."[12] In a nearly unprecedented move, the holder of these leases suddenly withdrew them.

This is just one example of the way the voices of local people, along with the Krug Memorandum and the resulting Jackson Hole Stipulation, set a precedent. Their influence was important in later efforts by citizens to stop energy development on USFS land in the Hoback Basin.

Between 1981 and 1988, a number of applications to drill followed. Exploratory wells appeared in numerous parts of the Hoback River watershed: lower Granite Creek, Cliff Creek, Shoal Creek, Kilgore Creek, Elk Ridge, South Fork Fisherman Creek, and The Rim of Hoback Basin. From a cabin we had rented in the Hoback Basin in the late 1980s, we could hear intermittent explosions echoing. We were told a company was drilling for gas, and a steady stream of trucks verified it. All wells were capped, either as dry holes or otherwise

FIGURE 26. A series of rectangular clear-cuts from the 1970s and narrow "leave strips," viewed from the Wyoming Peak Trail north of the Tri-Basin Divide. Forestry practices such as clear-cutting created controversy that led to passage of the National Forest Management Act in 1976. Photo: Susan Marsh.

FIGURE 27. The peaks of the Gros Ventre Wilderness loom over Cache Creek near the area where industry wanted to drill an exploratory oil well in 1980. Photo: Susan Marsh.

unpromising for immediate development. The drill sites were replanted with a nonnative seed mix that makes them stand out decades later. Most of the access roads remain open to the public for recreation. The BTNF used some to harvest commercial timber and later converted them to trails.

Though some leasing and drilling occurred during this time, the BTNF fell behind in completing the necessary environmental analysis, which delayed drilling proposals. This was partly because the specialists needed to conduct the analysis had been reassigned to complete the forest plan.

With increasing demand for energy, companies were anxious to develop reserves that promised profit, and the USFS and BLM were pressured to lease as much federal land with minerals as possible. Congress tried to keep up with competing demands for energy development on one hand and restraint from a public increasingly critical of developing public land for private gain on the other. It responded in 1987 with the passage of the Federal Onshore Oil and Gas Leasing Reform Act. This act required the USFS and BLM to share responsibility for authorizing oil and gas development within national forests. The USFS was directed to decide which lands were appropriate for leasing through its various forest plans. As it happened, regulations to implement this law were finalized in early 1990, the same time the BTNF completed its forest plan.

FIGURE 28. The confluence of Granite and Little Granite
Creeks, another area proposed for exploratory drilling in 1980.
Photo: Susan Marsh.

FIGURE 29. Smooth brome and yellow sweet clover were planted to restore this site after an exploratory well was drilled in 1981. These nonnative plants continue to dominate more than thirty years later. Photo: Susan Marsh.

IN THE MID-1980S, I met and married Paul Shepard, a scholar and professor of human ecology and natural philosophy at Pitzer College in Claremont, California. My life acquired a new trajectory with a focus on travel, research, and writing. On faculty exchanges and sabbaticals, we often lived abroad for months at a time, but we spent summers in the Hoback Basin, first renting a small cabin and in 1990 building our own, where we hoped to spend a good portion of our retirement years. Although I helped gather signatures for declaring the Hoback a wild and scenic river, I gave up most activism because of our travel schedule.

Each summer as we drove to and from our cabin, Paul and I noticed a remarkable change taking place in the Green River Basin. The roads were crowded with eighteen-wheel tankers and trucks hauling equipment for drilling and oil. Derricks sprang up like mushrooms on the sagebrush steppe, and the air was often so polluted that the Wyoming, Gros Ventre, and Wind River Ranges and the Uinta Mountains were barely visible through the haze. I asked a salesperson at a store in Big Piney if she could ever see the mountains. She replied, "Only occasionally on a very windy day."

4

Drill, Baby, Drill
(1990–2006)

THE STEAMROLLER ENERGY PRODUCTION IN the Green River Basin caught residents by surprise. The magnitude and pace of industrialization caused them to question the procedures for exploring and extracting oil and natural gas as well as the federal agencies' practices of leasing on public lands. Although the development at the Jonah Field, and later the Pinedale Anticline, took place primarily on BLM rangeland, the geologic structures with potential for oil and gas extended into the BTNF. The publication of the BTNF forest plan in 1990 was well timed since it clearly stated the procedures for energy exploration within the national forest, as well as a protocol for identifying and monitoring acceptable leasing areas.

Applying the protocols to the developing situation in the Green River Basin was not so easy because horizontal drilling and fracking increasingly complicated governmental monitoring of burgeoning energy development and production. According to author Richard Heinberg, these techniques for increasing oil and gas production "pose a danger not just to local water and air quality, but also to sound energy policy, and therefore to our collective ability to avert the greatest human-made economic and environmental catastrophe in history."[1]

In his book *Snake Oil: How Fracking's False Promise of Plenty Imperils Our Future,* Heinberg details the complex methodology; the massive amounts of equipment, materials and water; and the environmental consequences of fracking an oil or natural gas well, as well as the steps a company with mineral leases must negotiate to drill test wells. Included in the agreement to buy leases is permission to build roads, drilling pads, and pipelines; disrupt ongoing land use; "take millions of gallons of water from wells on the lands or rivers nearby"; and store or dispose of waste water. Sixty tractor-trailer loads of equipment and four to six tanker loads of water and fracking fluids are needed to clear vegetation from an area about the size of a football field and construct a 120-foot-tall platform with drilling equipment. After drilling and fracking, it takes several days to pump the fluid back into the ground or store it

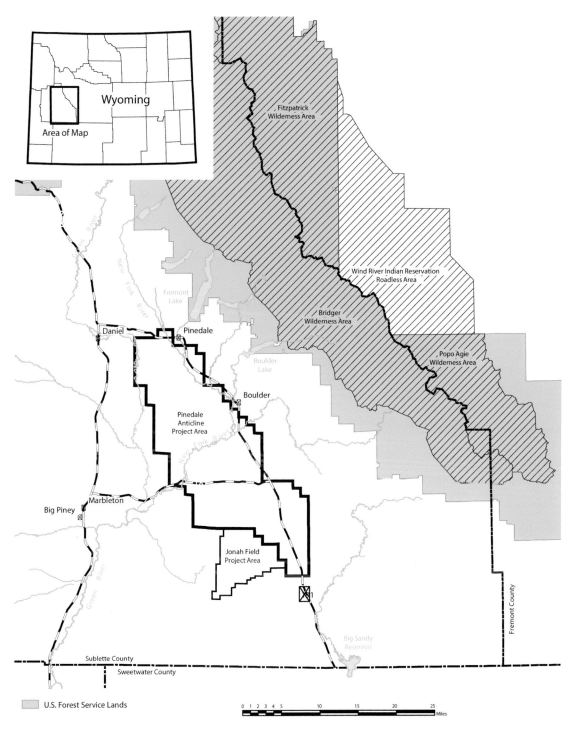

Wyoming

Area of Map

Fitzpatrick
Wilderness Area

Wind River Indian Reservation
Roadless Area

Bridger
Wilderness Area

Popo Agie
Wilderness Area

Fremont
Lake

Daniel

Pinedale

Boulder
Lake

Boulder

Pinedale
Anticline
Project Area

New Fork River

Marbleton

Big Piney

Jonah Field
Project Area

Green River

Big Sandy
Reservoir

Fremont County

Sublette County
Sweetwater County

U.S. Forest Service Lands

0 1 2 3 4 5   10   15   20   25
Miles

MAP 5. Map showing the locations of the Pinedale Anticline
and the Jonah Field in the upper Green River Basin. Map
courtesy of the BLM.

FIGURE 30. An artist's pallet of "produced water," a byproduct of fracking, in various settling ponds near the upper Green River. Photo by Bruce Gordon, courtesy of EcoFlight.

for future use or disposal. If natural gas is discovered, a nearby pipeline will be joined or a new one built. If oil is the product, trucks will haul it to a processing station. "Each well will have generated 1,800 to 2,500 18-wheel truck trips."[2]

Fracking had been used since 1949 and was widespread by the 1970s in conventional wells. However, this method could not be used to extract petroleum products in rock strata such as sandstone or shale. In the early 1980s, George P. Mitchell of the Mitchell Energy & Development Corporation found that adding certain ingredients to the water and increasing the pressure during fracking could release natural gas. Energy companies developed their own ingredients for fracking, and, during exploration, they searched for "plays," productive strata for oil or gas extraction, and "sweet spots," areas where oil or gas had pooled and was easily accessible.

By the late 1980s, companies began directional drilling that made it possible to drill as many as seventeen wells from a single pad. Because of the increased production that resulted from fracking, directional drilling became a standard part of production. Development of 3-D imaging techniques optimized the success of identifying productive plays of gas and oil, and fracking greatly increased the flow and production. In the early 1990s, while government agencies were still developing likely scenarios for energy development based on older methods of production, fracking had already changed the game.

IN 1991, THE McMurry Oil Company, owned by W. M. McMurry, his son, Neil McMurry, and John Martin of Casper, Wyoming, turned its attention to production of natural gas, which was being touted as a clean fuel and—due to fracking—had become more economical. McMurry Oil began looking for prospects throughout the country. Ed Warner, the company's geologist, found an ideal location: the Jonah Field in Wyoming's Green River Basin. The company purchased mineral leases and three abandoned wells on 25,000 acres where the Presidio Oil Company had previously drilled without commercial success. Near the abandoned wells was an old pipeline that connected to the Opal facility, forty miles away. The Opal facility was soon to connect to the Kern River pipeline, then under construction, which ran almost a thousand miles to Bakersfield, California.

The owners of the McMurry Oil Company consulted James Shaw, a petroleum engineer, to help direct fracking. In 1993, to their amazement, the three abandoned wells produced two million cubic feet of natural gas per day. This was the spark that ignited the rush for natural gas production on the Pinedale Anticline and the Jonah Field. Natural gas was already being produced in the area, but without a major pipeline to markets or the widespread use of fracking that increased the quantity, production had not been economically profitable until this time.[3]

As rising ozone levels and water pollution began to follow drilling, fracking became a dirty

FIGURE 31. One of the larger support facilities in the upper Green River Basin. These include "man camps," which house workers on-site. Photo by Bruce Gordon, courtesy of EcoFlight.

FIGURE 32. An apparent attempt to reclaim a well pad in the Jonah Field. The ground appears to have been cultivated, though the vegetation is mostly weeds: Russian thistle and lamb's quarters. Photo by Linda Baker, courtesy of EcoFlight.

word, and its ill effects did not escape the notice of the residents of the Hoback Basin. Unlike the sweeping open country of the Green River Basin, they lived in a small, enclosed mountain valley surrounded by high peaks with a single source of water—they knew air and water pollution would be disastrous.

IN THOSE EARLY years when energy exploration began spreading over western Wyoming,

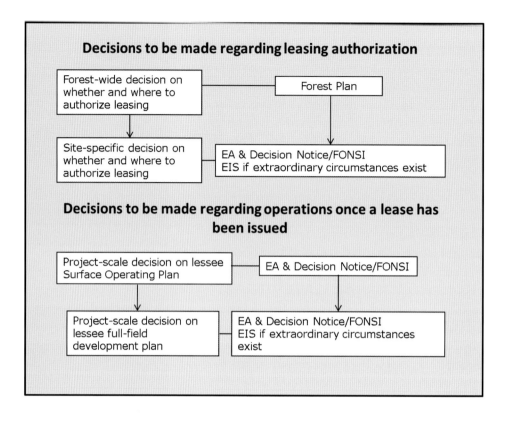

ordinary citizens did not have the kind of information about its effects that we have today. They only knew what they saw: reduced visibility and increasing air pollution, deterioration of their local cultural milieu, and negative impact on the wildlife and its habitat that was part of their heritage. Increasingly they read or heard about health problems that resulted from toxic pollutants that appeared in the water of people living in areas of energy production. Small rural communities in the upper Green River Basin, however, continued to welcome expanding energy development because it promised prosperity. By the late 1990s, as the rate of exploration and development exploded, and signs of a deteriorating landscape became apparent, one and all began voicing concerns. Industrialization, like a wild horse being tamed for riding, had suddenly broken loose and ran away with the bit in its mouth—a drill bit.

One of the people alarmed by the rapidly changing landscape is Linda Baker, who started the Upper Green River Alliance, a group seeking to protect water and air quality, wildlife habitat, and the human environment in the face of rapid energy development. As someone who lives in the midst of the development, Linda has seen the consequences firsthand. "Oil and gas are Wyoming's bread and butter," she told me in an interview in October 2013.

Now that the boom has busted, the state is saying, "Oh, gee! Maybe we could have gotten more money from those leases or from the gases that flared and vented into the air. What are we going to do about that winter habitat that we lost? Maybe we might try to bring fertilizer into it; maybe we will just spend all of our mitigation money on conservation easements and call it good because we can't think of anything else to do." It's criminal, and it's heartbreaking, and it's not going to end.

While the BLM oversaw energy development in its gas-rich upper Green River Basin, industry began to express increasing interest in national forest lands to the north and west. BTNF staff, including forest supervisor Brian Stout (who retired in 1994), had a strong desire to see provisions outlined in the 1990 forest plan put into effect. That plan was considered unusual for both its progressive language and the degree to which the public was involved in its preparation. It was the only forest plan in the Intermountain Region that was not delayed by lawsuits.

The Federal Onshore Oil and Gas Leasing Reform Act had given the USFS authority to make four types of decisions related to energy leasing: two defined where and how leasing could occur within national forests, and two related to operations. Chronologically and with increasing levels of detail, they are the following:

(1) A large-scale decision on availability, completed as part of the forest plan;

(2) Site-specific decisions as to how and where leasing restrictions and stipulations should be applied;

(3) Site-specific approval of surface operating plans after the lease is granted;

(4) Approval of surface operating plans for full field development in the case of a discovery.[4]

Soon after the forest plan was published, the BTNF began to implement the second step of this process. The oil and gas industry identified areas of interest, and the BTNF prioritized them for analysis. Management areas (MAs) 25 and 26 on the east slope of the Wyoming Range where the

Riley Ridge gas and helium development already existed were the first of a dozen areas considered between 1990 and 1993.

At this point, the number of applications for leases and workload had grown so rapidly that it was more than the BTNF staff could respond to in a timely manner. In 1995, when a considerable backlog had accumulated, energy companies sued the USFS for not taking action. The agency, spurred by the lawsuit, began an intensive effort to complete the environmental assessments.

One of these was launched in 1997, when the BTNF initiated an analysis covering 376,000 acres in four MAs, including the Hoback Basin (MA 21), Moccasin Basin (MA 45), Union Pass (MA 71), and the upper Green River Basin (MA 72). Inventoried Roadless areas inventoried during the RARE II process, grizzly bear habitat, eligible wild and scenic rivers, and emerging concerns about deteriorating air quality in the upper Green River Basin were issues the staff expected to address before the analysis began, and because of these and other extraordinary circumstances within the four MAs, the USFS dispensed with the usual environmental assessment and began immediately producing an EIS.

The USFS did not underestimate the level of controversy and complexity associated with this project. The EIS went through a lengthy series of revisions during its preparation and reviews, and the record of decision was not published until 2003. (The record of decision is the final step in the NEPA process when an EIS is written, stating the alternative chosen and the reasons for selecting it.) Between the commencement of work on the EIS and the final record of decision, a succession of forest supervisors and staff came and went, causing delays. In the record of decision, Forest Supervisor Kniffy Hamilton, who had come to the BTNF four years before, stated her decision in a letter to the BLM state director "not to authorize the BLM to issue oil and gas leases at this

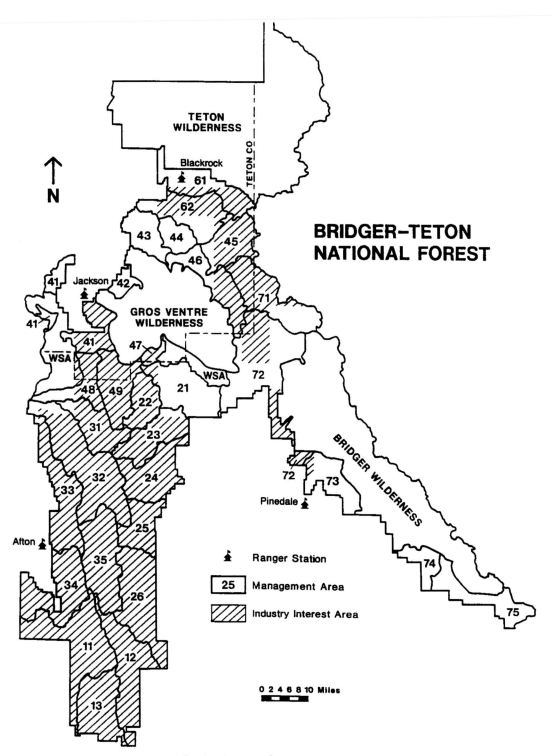

MAP 6. The management areas defined in the BTNF forest plan. Industry identified the shaded areas as the ones they were most interested in. Map courtesy of the USFS.

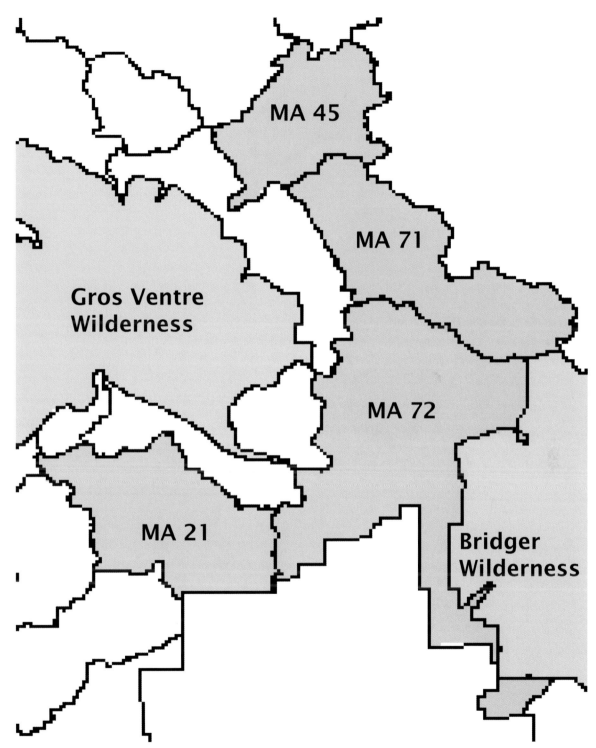

MAP 7. The four management areas (MAs) studied for the BTNF's oil and gas environmental impact statement, 1997–2003. MA 21 is the Hoback Basin. Map courtesy of the USFS.

time in Management Areas 21, 45, 71, and 72 of the Bridger-Teton National Forest in Wyoming."[5] The words "at this time" left open the possibility for authorizing the BLM to issue leases later, and her decision applied only to new leases. Those already granted were not affected, and holders had the right to develop them. There were many existing valid leases in MA 21, the Hoback Basin.

IN FEBRUARY 2004, the USFS announced that it was authorizing the BLM to lease 175,000 acres of national forest lands on the east slope of the Wyoming Range. A wellspring of protests rose. The announcement was the catalyst that alarmed all constituencies, from outfitters to wildlife experts, ranchers, business owners, residents, AFL-CIO members who worked in southwestern Wyoming's mines and gas fields (and who spent their time off in the Wyoming Range), and public officials. People valued their public lands. They could see what had happened to BLM lands in the upper Green River Basin, and they did not want their national forest to be destroyed in the same manner.

Many had interpreted the 2003 decision regarding the four MAs to the north as a hopeful sign that BTNF management was sensitive to the potentially harmful effects of gas development in the forest. Now it seemed that they had been wrong.

Prior to making the announcement, the BTNF prepared what it called a supplemental information report where it stated that the post–forest plan environmental assessments done between 1990 and 1993 were adequate and did not require revision. The report acknowledged three new issues: the USFWS's proposed listing of the Canada lynx as threatened, newly available information about air quality, and the potential need for an updated development scenario. In spite of this, the BTNF determined that these issues had been adequately addressed in the existing environmental assessments.[6]

Many contested the conclusion in the supplemental information report that leasing 175,000 acres for oil and gas development would have no effect on air quality or threatened species. And a number of important conditions had changed since the environmental assessments in the early 1990s. They had not included development scenarios, as required. The 2001 Roadless Area Conservation Rule, enacted well after the original assessments had been completed, was not mentioned in the report. (The roadless rule restricted road building within inventoried roadless areas, and much of the 175,000 acres about to be leased lay within one of several roadless areas.) The report paid no attention to cumulative impact that had occurred since the early 1990s, including the pace and extent of development in the upper Green River Basin.

ON THE HEELS of the BTNF announcement came another piece of news that produced great concern, especially to the residents of the Hoback Basin: Texas-based Plains Exploration & Production Company (PXP) had purchased a block of existing leases in the Hoback and Noble Basins. It seemed to many as if a large part of the BTNF might soon become the locus for much industrial activity.

Between 2004 and 2005, individuals and organizations began to organize to fight this occurrence. This was not a natural coalition that resulted from shared values. Some people were wary of others because of their own perceptions as well as stereotypical biases about the groups involved: ranchers, conservationists, outfitters, sportspeople, entrepreneurs, politicians.

The participants came to the table with diverse opinions, but all were united in their understanding that energy development—if conducted as it had been in the upper Green River Basin—would devastate the Hoback and the backcountry of the Wyoming Range that residents,

FIGURE 34. View north from Bare Pass on the eastern front of the Wyoming Range. The BTNF lands below Triple and Lander Peaks on the skyline are part of the original 175,000 acres approved for energy leasing by the USFS in 2004. Photo: Susan Marsh.

anglers, hunters, and campers loved. The various players can be grouped into larger categories that are typical in environmental conflicts like this one:

(1) Individuals who took action as circumstances or their consciences dictated;

(2) Nongovernmental organizations (NGOs). Most were long-established national and state conservation and wildlife groups. Other groups developed locally in response to this particular controversy, often initiated by people whose property, livelihood, or recreational interests depended on healthy and diverse wildlands in the Wyoming Range and Hoback Basin;

(3) Public officials who had direct influence over the process and chose to work with citizens in negotiations or through legislation;

(4) Philanthropists whose mission was to preserve western lands and wildlife in the Rockies.

Before any collaboration among the constituencies commenced, some individuals began taking action on their own. Among the first to become involved independently was Rollin (Rollie) D. Sparrowe, a retired wildlife biologist; with his wife, Bettina, he had moved to Daniel, Wyoming, full time in 2003. They have a cabin in the Hoback Basin. I interviewed him in November 2013.

Rollie had held a position in the Wildlife Research Unit of the USFWS for more than twenty years. While with the USFWS, he was the federal official in charge of establishing the Wyoming Cooperative Fish and Wildlife Research Unit, a collaborative effort linking the University of Wyoming, the Wyoming Game and Fish Department, the Wildlife Management Institute, and the USFWS. Because of this agreement, as well as studies in the past on elk and deer populations, data in the upper Green River Basin have been collected over an extended period of time.

As energy development accelerated in the upper Green River Basin during the 1990s, Rollie—then president of the Wildlife Management Institute in Washington, DC—assembled members of professional associations to develop plans to lessen the impact on wildlife and fisheries. They presented their conclusions to energy companies and the U.S. Department of the Interior, specifying steps such as slowing the pace, planning carefully, studying changes from the baseline data available, and—after careful analysis each year—making changes to lessen the impact of development.

Rollie's group was told that the current scale and pace of energy development would not allow the BLM to implement such plans. Instead, they were advised to submit their comments as part of the public participation process under NEPA. They did so, but their substantive recommendations were largely ignored.

FIGURE 35. Rollin and Bettina Sparrowe. Rollie tried for decades to encourage energy development at a slow, sustainable pace. Photo courtesy of Rollie Sparrowe.

"I've commented on development plans and projects in the upper Green River Basin for seventeen years now," Rollie told me. "I've never seen a meaningful change."

In 2000–2001, energy production ramped up in the Pinedale Anticline, 80 percent of which lay on BLM land. Citizens were alarmed by the rapid spread of development on public land, and the anticline was close to their homes and upwind of the Bridger Wilderness. The BLM responded to public concern by forming the Pinedale Anticline Working Group (PAWG), a citizens' advisory committee. Rollie was among the members of this group and led the wildlife committee for a time. At first, members were optimistic that they might have some influence, but they quickly became jaded as the BLM made it clear that their recommendations would not be taken seriously.

"I happened to focus on wildlife, which was my expertise," Rollie said.

So it was quite controversial because the substantive recommendations were ignored by BLM. The deer herd had started its decline, and industry acknowledged that there was a problem. A committee that included industry recommended to [the] BLM that they get the right people together to look at the data to see what was happening and try to figure out what we could do differently. They stonewalled it for nine months and then gave me the answer that no, we can't do that. We hadn't asked them to do anything very profound, so that was enough for a lot of the people here.

The group began to dissolve, and some people walked out of meetings in disgust. One person reported overhearing BLM employees saying they wished the working group would just go away. After a while, they did.

After his experience with the PAWG and his many other efforts to influence BLM policy, Rollie stopped trying to offer suggestions. But as the Hoback Basin became directly threatened, he had no choice but to rejoin the fray. He had seen—by 2004—the way energy development in the upper Green River Basin had consumed the landscape and its small towns.

Rollie is doubtful that the damage done in the upper Green River Basin can be mitigated. "My wife and I bought a cabin on The Rim," he said. "We can see the whole Wind River Range from our front porch. I was up there this autumn for hunting, and it's a rare day when we don't have a lot of pollution."

When I talked with her in October 2013, Linda Baker of the Upper Green River Alliance underscored Rollie's experience with the PAWG. "Thirty-six million dollars was put up for mitigation," she said. However, little of that money was used to moderate impacts to air, water, and wildlife, which was the intention. Rather, the funds purchased conservation easements from private

landowners. "It enriched a handful of people at the rest of our expense," Linda observed.

Linda Cooper prepared lunch for me as I sat at the kitchen island in her home at Hoback Ranches in August 2013. I had been there before. In 2005, she had held information meetings for the communities that would be affected by new leases and proposed energy development nearby. A network of concerned and informed people began to coalesce and grow as the battle continued.

Linda was alarmed about leasing on the east front of the Wyoming Range. "It would have created an industrial corridor from Merna to the upper Hoback River," she said. While monitoring the proposal, Linda was one of the first residents of the Hoback Basin to organize for a fight against the Eagle Prospect proposal. She created Stop Drilling—Save the Bridger-Teton (SDSBT), a citizen-action group. As a business consultant, she had broad experience in both public and private-sector work. Abandoning his vow to shun further meetings, Rollie Sparrowe joined her efforts to inform the local and broader community of the pending dangers of natural gas development. Enlisting wildlife biologists, civil engineers, and air-quality scientists, SDSBT armed itself.

Linda observed that after World War II, energy was treated as a commodity. Energy companies and individuals could make money and position themselves by trading leases, as she put it, "without dipping a stick in the ground." The more leases available, the more chances for holders to make a profit if oil or gas was discovered.

John Lockridge was one broker who held leases on both public and private land. After twenty years, he held most of the leases in the Merna–Hoback Basin area. In 2004, he sold his holdings to PXP. The BLM unitized the various leases formerly held by Lockridge. (With unitization, all of PXP's leases were given the same

The Wyoming Game and Fish Department has designated the Hoback Basin as a crucial habitat priority area, needed by moose, pronghorn, mule deer, and elk for migration corridors, calving sites, and both summer and winter range. It provides habitat for two native cutthroat trout subspecies—the Colorado River cutthroat and the Snake River fine-spotted cutthroat—and supports amphibians, songbirds, small mammals, and raptors.

A female greater sage grouse forages in winter. Photo: Susan Marsh.

A mule-deer doe browses on snowbush, also favored by elk. Photo: Susan Marsh.

A bull moose wanders through sagebrush between stands of willow and cottonwood. Photo: Susan Marsh.

Pronghorn migrate in small groups between the Hoback Basin and upper Green River. Photo: Susan Marsh.

FIGURE 36. Linda Cooper, founder of Stop Drilling—Save the Bridger-Teton (SDSBT). Photo courtesy of Linda Cooper.

consisted of 23,260 acres, including 10,927 acres of BTNF land, 240 acres managed by the BLM, 80 acres of land owned by the state, and 12,013 acres of private land, about 5,000 of which lay under Hoback Ranches.[7] Using directional drilling, PXP could drill underneath part of the residential subdivision. The people who lived there were most worried about the threat to water. The limited amount of surface water was a vital resource for people and wildlife. Groundwater was the source of many domestic wells.

Recognizing the risk, Linda went to the Pinedale BLM office in November 2005. She told me that she put the BLM on notice that there would be a fight. "This is wrong," she told them. "This is never going to happen."

PRIOR TO 2004, many national, state, and regional environmental organizations had become involved in the controversy over energy production in the upper Green River Basin. However, the national groups had taken a cautious approach out of respect for local communities and their desire to manage their own affairs. But when the USFS announced it was going to authorize the BLM to lease 175,000 acres in the Wyoming Range, these organizations jumped into the battle. They began to share resources and information and work more closely together. These groups included TWS, the Greater Yellowstone Coalition (GYC), the WOC, Trout Unlimited (TU), the National Outdoor Leadership School (NOLS), the Jackson Hole Conservation Alliance, Earthjustice, the Biodiversity Conservation Alliance, the Natural Resources Defense Council, the Sierra Club, the Upper Green River Alliance, American Rivers, the Wyoming Audubon Society, the Murie Center, the Wyoming Wilderness Association, and the Wyoming Wildlife Federation.

Out of this impressive group of NGOs, some people emerged to take leadership. Among the first was Peter Aengst, senior director of the

ten-year period based on the most recent one.) Unitization provided benefits for the company: in addition to giving PXP more time to explore for and develop minerals, it facilitated the company's ability to manage multiple leases. Directional drilling, along with hydraulic fracturing, would potentially give the company broader access to mineral resources beyond the geographic area of its leases.

When Linda Cooper learned what PXP had done after acquiring the leases west of Hoback Ranches, she became alarmed. The original area that PXP proposed for exploratory drilling

Northern Rockies office of TWS, based in Bozeman, Montana; I interviewed him in October 2013. In 2001, he had accepted the assignment as TWS's Northern Rockies oil and gas coordinator.

Oil and gas production was in full swing, and the emphasis on energy development had intensified at the national level. President George W. Bush had named an energy task force headed by Vice President Dick Cheney. Cheney had been CEO of Halliburton, an oil-field services company, from 1995 to 2000. The primary focus of the energy task force was not on conservation or energy independence but on increasing the flow of oil to the United States from suppliers abroad. At the same time, there was an increased effort to produce oil and natural gas on large tracts of public lands in Wyoming, Montana, Colorado, and New Mexico.

Peter soon focused his attention on the 175,000 acres the BTNF was about to authorize the BLM to lease. Because the bulk of the land was within inventoried roadless areas, including the 315,000-acre Grayback Roadless Area, TWS was keenly interested in the controversy.

He told me that there were places in Wyoming and Montana that were going to be under threat because of the Bush administration's interest. Given the national pressure on forest supervisors at the time, "Kniffy Hamilton felt like she had to go forward," Peter told me.

A broad array of organizations and citizens joined Peter in his opposition to the BTNF leasing plan. Regardless of political-party affiliation, or whether they lived in Sublette or Teton County, were employed in the present or past by oil or mining industries, were skilled workers or owned businesses or ranches, were longtime residents or newcomers, they joined to fight the BTNF proposal.

One of Peter Aengst's early collaborators was Lloyd Dorsey, program associate with the GYC in Jackson. Lloyd possessed deep knowledge and

FIGURE 37. Peter Aengst, who was oil and gas coordinator of the Northern Rockies office of the Wilderness Society. Photo courtesy of Peter Aengst.

appreciation for wild animals and their habitats in Wyoming. He was also a natural partner and respectful of other opinions. During his tenure with GYC, he hired, trained, and mentored young environmentalists who moved on to influential positions in other organizations. Lloyd and GYC acted as mediator and facilitator at problem solving and collaborative meetings of those working to prevent energy development in the Wyoming Range and Hoback Basin.

Lloyd joined Peter Aengst to formulate a survey of attitudes of voters in Sublette County, which encompasses both the Green River and

FIGURE 38. Beaver pond in Pass Creek on the eastern slope of the Wyoming Range, part of the area that the USFS approved for energy leasing. Photo: Susan Marsh.

FIGURE 39. Lloyd Dorsey, a sportsman and longtime environmental advocate. His work with the Greater Yellowstone Coalition in Jackson included facilitating meetings and mentoring young conservationists. Photo courtesy of Lloyd Dorsey.

Hoback Basins. The results of the survey indicated that most voters were not opposed to energy development. They believed that oil and gas drilling would not affect wildlife negatively and would improve the economy of the region. Although voters agreed that environmental conditions had worsened, they were convinced that it was their duty to themselves and the nation to develop oil and gas resources. What concerned them was the influx of new residents that would change the local culture and increase taxes. The results of the survey did not indicate a populace poised to fight energy development. Peter and Lloyd realized they had much work to do to convince locals that prime ecosystems in Wyoming were under threat.

MEANWHILE, WYOMING'S SENIOR senator, Craig Thomas, had been holding town meetings in western Wyoming to get a sense of the public's attitudes toward energy development. One of his field representatives was Patti Smith, who served as his eyes and ears in five counties in Wyoming, including Sublette County, where the energy boom was under way. She told me, when I interviewed her in July 2013, that Senator Thomas had joined her to tour the Jonah Field and the Pinedale Anticline in January 2003. This gas field had gone into full development three years earlier. Afterward he had remarked that these were probably good places to drill for natural gas.

Public concern about the BTNF announcement to authorize leasing on the east side of the Wyoming Range had reached his office through Patti and other staff members; he realized he needed to see this area as well.

Senator Thomas was not one to take vacations; his idea of a holiday was to ride horseback into the mountains. So in the summer of 2004, when Forest Supervisor Kniffy Hamilton invited him on a pack trip into the Wyoming Range, he accepted. Many of us in the Hoback Basin gathered at St. Hubert the Hunter Church in Bondurant to meet Senator Thomas as the pack train prepared to leave for the mountains. It was reassuring to know that they would be riding into the Wyoming Range, where they could begin to understand our concerns more completely.

Patti recalled that, standing around the campfire in Roosevelt Meadows one evening, Thomas had asked Hamilton in his very low voice, "Now why would you want to lease these lands?" He continued to ask pointed questions concerning the slope of the land, the impact on wildlife, the depth that would be drilled, how much water would be required, and if air pollution would become a problem. That the mountainsides were steep and the water and air were pure did not escape his notice. After the pack trip, Thomas remarked to Patti that drilling in the national forest might not be the right thing to do.

He reiterated this sentiment a month later in a statement to the *Jackson Hole News & Guide* and at a meeting in Jackson with state legislators and county commissioners. He told them, "We must work to ensure that the natural beauty of the Bridger-Teton National Forest is protected. This area supports a wide variety of wildlife and has many outstanding features. In addition, since the forest is in close proximity to Grand Teton

FIGURE 40. Senator Craig Thomas supported energy development in general but questioned drilling in the Wyoming Range. Before his death, he drafted legislation to protect the area from future development. Photo from United States Congress, public domain.

National Park, we must make sure this area is well protected."[8]

This simple statement carried great weight with the public. Diverse groups and individuals, many of whom were already working to oppose leases in the Wyoming Range, began to explore broader possibilities through legislation. They saw an important ally in Senator Thomas, someone who had the potential to protect the entire Wyoming Range from further energy development.

In September 2004, a month after Senator Thomas's pack trip, Governor Dave Freudenthal invited a group of county commissioners, state legislators, grazing-association members, Wyoming Game and Fish Department officials, and

FIGURE 41. Roosevelt Meadows, where Senator Thomas and Supervisor Kniffy Hamilton camped during a pack trip in August 2004. Photo: Susan Marsh.

BTNF personnel to meet with him on-site. Peter Aengst, who represented environmental interests at this gathering, described that memorable day in our interview:

> Governor Fruedenthal was going to do an overflight with Game and Fish. Then he would land, and we'd meet him in Bondurant. We were going to drive up Cliff Creek and the upper Hoback and talk about the values of the Wyoming Range.

> But the governor's motorcade arrived in a downpour, which foiled plans for an overflight as well as the trip to Cliff Creek.

"We all drove up the upper Hoback to the end of the road and got out in the rain," Peter said. One of the people who had been invited because he had been a financial supporter of the governor was Hans Graf, and he had a home nearby. Graf invited the group to go back to his house. His wife, Molly, was taken by surprise when twenty people barged in, but she quickly provided lunch.

At the gathering, the governor wanted to hear from the USFS first. Peter said the BTNF representative justified leasing and told the group it wasn't such a big deal. Then the governor asked to hear the conservation side. He turned to State Senate Republican Grant Larson, who gave a

FIGURE 42. View across aspen stands to the crest of the Wyoming Range from North Horse Creek, near Gary Amerine's home. Photo: Susan Marsh.

very passionate and compelling speech. From the long-term standpoint, this was not the place to be leasing, Larson said. He urged the governor to think about the next generation and what had been fueling the economy.

After Larson spoke, Fruedenthal launched into a complete attack on the USFS, which—from Peter's point of view—was very powerful. The governor ended by saying, "I will fight this to my dying day."

In October, the BTNF announced that it had withdrawn its plan to authorize leasing 175,000 acres in the Wyoming Range. After eliminating inventoried roadless areas from the lands to be leased, the BTNF had reduced the acreage to

44,720 acres. Since this area was already accessible by existing roads, BTNF officials assumed the adjusted acreage would no longer be controversial. They were incorrect.

AMONG THOSE INVITED to the governor's meeting in September 2004 was Gary Amerine, owner of Greys River Trophies, a big-game outfitting and guiding business and an active member of Wyoming Outfitters and Guides Association. The view from his home, where I interviewed him in October 2013, encompasses the eastern front of the Wyoming Range and the sagebrush steppe of the Green River Basin. Lush willow-clad Horse Creek emerges from the foothills and flows into

FIGURE 43. Gary Amerine, founder of Citizens Protecting the Wyoming Range (CPWR). Photo courtesy of Gary Amerine.

"We had over one hundred—that is, families. Some had several people," he told me. "All I had them do was try to craft one sentence about how important Horse Creek is. It went all the way from 'We played baseball there' to 'There's a rock there in the middle of the leases that was home plate.'"

Some guests were people of few words. But they were able to come up with this succinct statement: "They shouldn't do it."

Gary sent the letter to the BTNF. From that point on, he says, announcements appeared prominently on the front pages of newspapers. More outfitters, ranchers, conservationists, sportspeople, and union steel workers from southwestern Wyoming who hunted and fished in the Wyoming Range joined the protest.

Gary gave credit to Senator Thomas's statement of caution about energy leasing in the national forest. "That opened the door," he told me.

According to Chris Wood, CEO of TU, Thomas's statement also stirred his organization into action. TU was especially interested because the Wyoming Range harbors three subspecies of native cutthroat trout—fine-spotted Snake River cutthroat, Colorado River cutthroat, and Bonneville cutthroat—that could be threatened by energy development in the area. During our interview in September 2013, he asked, "Where else but in the Wyoming Range can you fish for three species of native trout that have existed for thousands of years?" It was an unparalleled resource.

TU assigned Tom Reed, the northwestern director of its Sportsmen's Conservation Project, to work with Joe Ricketts, a wealthy rancher on the upper Hoback River who had a strong interest in seeing the area protected. In the past, Reed had struck up a friendship with Senator Thomas. They both shared an interest in horses and enjoyed riding them in the backcountry. Reed is the author of *Give Me Mountains for My Horses*, and

the Green River through ranch meadows. This is the backyard for the Merna ranching community and an entrance into a popular recreation area in the Wyoming Range for local people and visitors from nearby states.

Concerned about the lack of public notice regarding the BTNF's plans for leasing in the Wyoming Range, Gary hosted a barbeque at his ranch and invited the community. His goal was to inform people of the plans for energy development in their home territory. Because of scant media coverage to that point—small notices buried on the last pages of local papers—it was shocking news to many. At the barbeque, Gary presented a letter to the BTNF supervisor and asked people to add personal notes.

he had given a copy to both of Wyoming's senators. Thomas had sent him a thank-you note for the gift.

Reed joined many others in hoping their friends in state and federal office would be able to help protect the Wyoming Range. "Gary Amerine and I took a lot of people out on horseback and showed them the Wyoming Range," Reed told me on the phone in March 2014. "I took a reporter for the Cheyenne paper and rode the length of the Wyoming Range: over a hundred miles, and we did it in nine days."

Individuals and members of conservation groups learned a lot about energy leasing and federal land management, and this information proved valuable in the year to come. Senator Thomas offered them some hope, yet the imminent threat of energy leasing on the east slope of the Wyoming Range remained. The BTNF proceeded with authorizing the BLM to offer leases within the 44,720 acres.

FIGURE 44. Tom Reed, who served as the northwestern director of Trout Unlimited's Sportsmen's Conservation Project. Photo courtesy of Trout Unlimited.

IN JUNE 2005, shortly after finishing law school, Lisa McGee joined WOC. WOC is Wyoming's oldest independent conservation group, founded in 1967 by Tom Bell and other environmentalists, including Mardy Murie. When she arrived at WOC, Lisa soon joined the efforts of Peter Aengst and Lloyd Dorsey, along with TU and NOLS, all of whom continued to oppose leasing on the east slope of the Wyoming Range.

Lisa—modest, quiet, and eager to give more credit to those she worked with than to herself— put her training and finely tuned attention to detail to work early with results that had far-reaching influence on protecting the Wyoming Range. In December 2005 and April 2006, when the BLM issued the first two of four leases within the 44,720 acres, Lisa and others filed protests. The agency denied the protests, stating, in effect, that if the BTNF considered the area appropriate for energy leasing, the BLM had no reason

to argue. After the second lease was issued, Lisa filed a request for stay of execution to the Interior Board of Land Appeals (IBLA) on behalf of WOC, NOLS, and a number of sportspeople's and conservation groups. The IBLA granted the stay and indicated appellants would likely be successful on the merits of their appeals. In response, the BLM upheld the protests on the final two sales, and all four leases were deferred. Meanwhile, the BLM requested a remand of the BTNF's leasing decision to remedy flaws in the environmental analysis.

"The IBLA granted the BLM's remand request," Lisa said in an interview in November 2013. "The Bridger-Teton agreed to consider changed circumstances in an updated environmental analysis. It was still being handled as an EA [environmental assessment] at the time."

Lisa told us the IBLA also stated that, based on the new analysis, it might be necessary for the BLM to cancel the leases, and the BLM

FIGURE 45. Lisa McGee of the Wyoming Outdoor Council. Lisa became one of the leaders in the PXP campaign as she ferreted out improprieties, legal missteps, and feigned amnesia of historical and legal precedents by both governmental agencies and corporations. Photo: Susan Marsh.

"DRILLING IN THE national forest may not be the right thing to do"—Senator Thomas might have been surprised to learn that a simple statement after a pack trip had such a galvanizing effect. Recreational hunters, anglers, and outfitter guides were propelled into activity by the prospect of seeing the Wyoming Range offered for energy leasing, as well as by Thomas's quote in the Jackson Hole newspaper. Commercial outfitters relied for their livelihood on vast public wildlands, and they questioned the wisdom of allowing energy development in the incomparable backcountry of the Wyoming Range with its hunting grounds and fishing streams. Members of the Wyoming Outfitters and Guides Association, Wyoming Wildlife Federation, and TU joined forces, and a citizen-action group was born.

While many were concerned primarily with the 44,720 acres in the Wyoming Range, Linda Cooper focused on the leases held by PXP. In 2005, her group, SDSBT, circulated a petition against drilling gas wells in the Hoback Basin. She collected a thousand names from across the United States.

In the campaign to stop drilling—thanks in part to the information provided by SDSBT—water became one of the primary concerns for residents of the Hoback Basin. Linda Cooper pointed out that the water in their wells and the Hoback River came from a sole-source aquifer, and little or no research had been done on the hydrogeology of the upper Hoback River watershed. Water quantity and quality were equally worrisome: extracting natural gas from just one well requires millions of gallons of water. In addition, evidence continued to mount that fracking contaminated groundwater.

Tom Darin, who had worked previously with Lloyd Dorsey and the GYC, was now a staff attorney and public-lands director for the Jackson Hole Conservation Alliance. As the name

acknowledged that the improperly issued leases from the first two sales might be voided. "The Forest Service decided at that point to go with a third party NEPA contractor to do the new analysis," she said. "And write an EIS."

Lisa's success should not be underestimated. Placing the leases on hold gave a reprieve to those concerned that the BTNF was rushing to lease the Wyoming Range. Now the agency would have to conduct a more complete EA before authorizing the BLM to lease more of the 44,720 acres. This would take time, allowing those concerned about energy leasing in the Wyoming Range to strategize and begin working together.

FIGURE 46. Autumn colors and clear blue waters characterize the lower Hoback River, which flows through a deep canyon below Bondurant. Thanks to legislation drafted by Senator Thomas, this section is a national recreational river. Photo: Susan Marsh.

implies, the organization focused primarily on issues in the immediate Jackson area. But Darin was also concerned about what was happening east of Jackson. The board of directors and the executive director of the alliance agreed with him, and they added what was happening in the Hoback Basin and Wyoming Range to their program agenda. As a result, Darin collaborated with Lloyd Dorsey on a presentation entitled "Bridger-Teton National Forest Leasing Proposal," which they presented in several communities. The program showcased the scenic, recreational, and wildlife values in the Wyoming Range that were threatened by energy development and offered suggestions about what could be done about it.

I attended their first meeting at the Teton County Library. Tim Preso, an attorney with Earthjustice, began the program, followed by Lloyd Dorsey and Tom Darin. I didn't stay for the discussion since I avoid driving to the cabin after dark because of the mule deer in the area.

I remember the drive back. By that time, I had joined Linda Cooper's efforts with SDSBT and was taking a more active role in opposing gas leasing. Although I had kept abreast of the controversy from the beginning, I had not participated actively because of my husband Paul's illness and—after his death—the task of editing his last books and assembling an archive.

Driving along that evening, as I reached the opening to Hoback Canyon, where Grayback Ridge meets the Gros Ventre Range, I was overcome with emotion. I felt such gratitude to these people who had taken up the cause and were informing the people of Jackson about the problem we were facing in Hoback Basin, an isolated community with a small population. This first public meeting in the Jackson area was important to inform these neighbors and enlist their support. As Tom Darin said when I talked to him, the alliance recognized the connections between Jackson Hole and Hoback Basin. Pronghorn and mule deer were among the species that migrated between them, and air flowed from Hoback Basin west to the Snake River, where any airborne pollutants from energy development would follow. Besides, Darin said, "We would not leave our friends out to dry."

5

The Perfect Storm
(2006–2010)

IN DECEMBER 2005, PXP FILED A NOTICE OF staking for Eagle Prospect. This notice turned the possibility of drilling by PXP into reality and sparked new resolve in those who opposed leasing or development in the Wyoming Range.

A month later, in January 2006, the BTNF issued a scoping letter on PXP's Eagle Prospect. The company proposed one well pad with up to three wells, along with associated roads and facilities. In addition, 7.3 miles of reconstructed roads and 4.2 miles of new roads would be needed.

The BTNF hosted two public meetings and solicited written comments. Some of these came from Lloyd Dorsey with attorneys Bruce Pendery and Lisa McGee on behalf of WOC, GYC, and the Jackson Hole Conservation Alliance.

This group listed many specific shortcomings in the scoping document. It did not adequately state the need to protect riparian and wetland areas, vegetation, and scenic quality. Neither did it identify the potential impact of increased traffic on wildlife or nearby residents and recreational visitors. The respondents claimed the document

relied on outdated baseline data and didn't consider the habitat needs for endangered species. Perhaps most importantly, they said the scoping document failed to mention a full-field development scenario. As part of Amendment 1, the BTNF's forest plan stated that the forest had to "project and analyze the type and amount of post-leasing activity that is reasonably foreseeable."[1] The scoping letter did not indicate whether this analysis would be done.

The Eagle Prospect aroused concern among those who had the Jonah Field in their rearview mirrors. They saw themselves headed down the same road to disastrous industrialization. When PXP's president, Jim Flores, described the possible future development as a "nice field right in the middle of the forest" in the Pinedale and Jackson newspapers, it only increased their fears.

It wasn't only PXP's importune statement that sounded an alarm. People living in the area were already feeling the effects of nearly 500 well pads in the Jonah Field near Pinedale, and in January 2006, the BLM published its final EIS on the

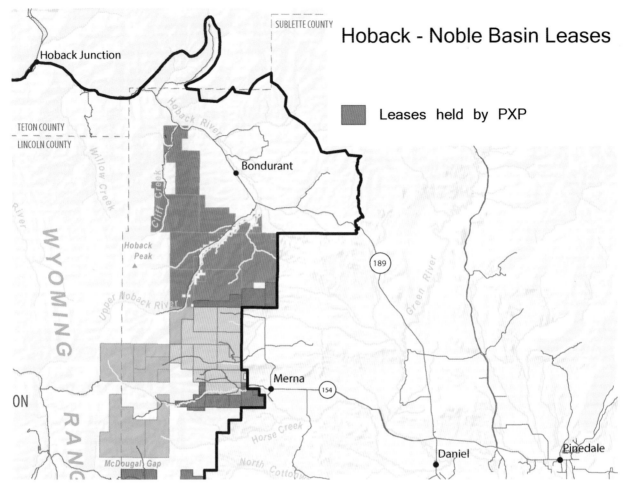

MAP 8. Detail of the Wyoming Range lease map. The leases shaded blue were retired as a result of the PXP buyout. Map courtesy of the Wyoming Outdoor Council.

so-called Jonah infill project, which would allow up to 3,100 additional wells in an area that was already highly developed. "It's been what I call the Jonah Creep," Linda Baker of the Upper Green River Alliance told me during our 2013 interview. "The Jonah Field started out with 37 wells, and then it went to 500, and then it went to 4,400."

Linda Cooper and SDSBT kept everyone informed by e-mail of ongoing developments. The time was right for a concentrated effort to push back before energy development consumed

the Hoback Basin as it had the upper Green River Basin.

While Linda Cooper and others prepared for the release of a draft environmental assessment of the Eagle Prospect, a group of sportspeople and outfitters—supported by Governor Freudenthal and Joe Ricketts, owner of a large parcel of private ranchland in the upper Hoback Valley—founded Citizens Protecting the Wyoming Range (CPWR), a local grassroots organization headed by outfitter Gary Amerine. CPWR began to seek

FIGURE 47. A calm autumn day on Monument Ridge in the Hoback Basin. Photo. Susan Marsh

national legislation to prevent any further mineral leasing in the Wyoming Range. GYC, TWS, WOC, and NOLS were among the organizations that joined them.

At this time, Stephanie (Steff) Kessler worked as the lead staff for GYC on Wyoming Range issues. Her connections to the Rocky Mountain region went back to the time when she was in college and hitchhiked to Wyoming to enroll as a student at NOLS, where she later became an instructor.

With the acumen to navigate both politics and activism, and her on-the-ground experience in Wyoming's wilderness, Steff had developed a deep understanding of Wyoming's outdoor values, communities, and politics. She has a finely tuned sense of timing when handling situations that are politically charged, and this sense served her well in the coming years.

While many others believed there was no chance of preventing PXP or any other company from developing its valid leases, Steff was strategizing for success. While others were willing to accept the impacts of inevitable development, Steff was busy developing a strategic approach that acknowledged the legality of the leases while challenging the company to live up to its promises and to offer the win-win solution of a lease buy-out.

IN JUNE OF 2006 conservationists, sportsmen, local citizens and other stakeholders met in Jackson Hole to discuss the status of the continuing threat of leasing in the Wyoming Range. After three hours of discussion, the group reached a consensus that federal legislation was needed to protect the Wyoming Range against future oil and gas leasing.

CPWR and other environmental organizations began actively building constituencies and refining their goals as momentum built and carried them through an increasingly complex landscape of citizen participation to protect the Wyoming Range. They lobbied Senator Thomas and other congressional members for legislation to obtain that protection.

Although all the groups were working toward national legislation to protect the Wyoming Range, they continued to pursue alternative methods of dealing with the undeveloped leases held by individuals and companies. As it began to seem inevitable that PXP would eventually develop its leases in the Hoback and Noble Basins, some members of CPWR began to talk with the company, hoping to influence the scale and effect of the development. Since the BTNF had not yet

COMMUNITIES OF PLANTS

As people come to know the Hoback Basin, each peak, ridge, and meadow reveals its singular character. Plants express an important part of that character: the scent of sagebrush after a summer rain, the sound of aspen leaves rustling in a breath of wind, the glory of summer wildflowers. The Hoback Basin's signature plant communities make it seem lovely to us and provide necessary food for wildlife.

Wetlands and streamside areas. Riparian zones, seeps and bogs, beaver ponds, and vernal pools lace the basin together into a necklace of water. Clear streams run from snowfields to collect in the basin, irrigating hay fields and providing homes for wildlife that ranges from frogs to moose.

Fringed gentian, a wetland obligate wildflower, growing beside Shoal Creek. Photo: Susan Marsh.

A high-elevation wetland near Fisherman Creek Lake with running water, still pools, and saturated soils of a wet meadow on its margins. Photo: Susan Marsh.

Sagebrush-bunchgrass steppe. Often overlooked as a drab foreground to the mountainsides above it, this plant community is vital to many songbirds, rodents, raptors, and mammals such as deer and pronghorn. Greater sage grouse eat little besides sagebrush, especially in winter when insects are scarce.

Aspen woodlands. The aspen is more than a tree. It develops an underground network of roots and shoots, resulting in stands that may extend several acres and are all the same plant community. Aspens offer homes for cavity-nesting birds and food for wildlife of all kinds.

Noble Basin offers ideal big-game habitat, a combination of sagebrush-bunchgrass steppe in the lower elevations, surrounded by mixed conifers, aspens, mountain shrubs, and willow wetlands. Photo: Susan Marsh.

Aspens in their fall finery frame The Sawtooth in upper Hoback Basin. Photo: Susan Marsh.

Clark Butte and the surrounding foothills host sagebrush mixed with grass and forbs, along with sedge meadows where water collects in the spring. Photo: Susan Marsh.

The bright lime green of new leaves cloaks Monument Ridge. Photo: Susan Marsh.

FIGURE 48. The Wilderness Society published "The Wyoming Range: Wyoming's Hidden Gem" in 2006. The twenty-nine-page booklet did much to raise awareness of the risk from energy development in a wild place. Courtesy of The Wilderness Society

produced an environmental document beyond the initial scoping notice in January 2006, the conservation coalition thought it was not the proper time to begin negotiating parameters for exploration and development. Their primary goal was to ward off industrialization of energy resources in the Hoback Basin.

As controversy over leasing the eastern slope of the Wyoming Range came to a head, publicity about the area increased in both Wyoming and Washington, DC. In 2006, TWS published and distributed a beautifully illustrated and factual

booklet, "The Wyoming Range: Wyoming's Hidden Gem," that described the biological, recreational, aesthetic, and economic benefits of the Wyoming Range.

In 2006, Ron Chilcote published *Wind River Wilderness*, a book that showcased the stunning landscapes of northwestern Wyoming, including the Wyoming Range. After his retirement from college teaching, Ron and his wife, Fran, settled in Hoback Ranches and continued publishing large-format photography books to raise awareness about wild landscapes deserving protection. *Wind River Wilderness* showcased their images, as well as those by leading photographers, along with essays and testimonials by regional authors. The National Resources Defense Council helped distribute a copy of the book to every congressperson in Washington. This book, along with wide media coverage, helped place the Wyoming Range on the map in Congress and across the country, as well as in Wyoming.

Around the same time, CPWR produced an informational brochure and map, "The Wyoming Range: Wyoming's Namesake Mountains." The map showed popular recreation areas and focused on places threatened by energy development. The cover stated that "responsible energy development means recognizing some places, such as the Wyoming Range, are too special to drill."

In the spring of 2007, CPWR released a two-part video, *The Wyoming Range: Too Special to Drill*. The film featured local citizens who spoke about what the range meant to them as ranchers, photographers, anglers, and hunters. Dustin Child, a local hunting outfitter, took clients into the eastern Wyoming Range, where some of them compared the area to other places where they had hunted. They said that, by far, the Wyoming Range was the most scenic and pristine. "I can't believe they're going to drill in God's country,"

FIGURE 49. The front and back covers of "The Wyoming Range: Wyoming's Namesake Mountains," published by CPWR. With a detailed map of the area on one side and information about the values at risk on the other, this brochure made the case that "enough is enough." Courtesy of Citizens Protecting the Wyoming Range.

one client told him. Child agreed that it was truly God's country. Responsible drilling, he said in the video, meant drilling in the right place at the right pace.[2]

WHEN TOM REED of TU began working with CPWR in 2007, he was assigned to help Joe Ricketts on the PXP issue. His directive was twofold: at the national level, he was to work for federal protection of the Wyoming Range. At the same time, he was to help negotiate an agreement with PXP for appropriate environmental protection and mitigation for any detrimental effects of full-field development resulting from the Eagle Prospect. Their deliberations were to be confidential until agreements had been reached. TU realized that the campaign had to start locally, rather than in the distant corners of Washington, DC. Chris Wood, the CEO of TU, described the process as traditional shoe-leather organizing. The primary goal was to protect the Wyoming Range from further mineral leasing.

CPWR began by polling people throughout the country to see how much they knew about the Wyoming Range. Interestingly, they found that—unlike the Front Ranges in Montana and Colorado—the Wyoming Range was unfamiliar to most of the general public. Ricketts instructed his public-relations person to describe the Wyoming Range as a "hidden gem" and publicized it nationwide.

TU created a shell organization called Sportsmen for the Wyoming Range to identify them as strong advocates to protect the Wyoming Range. Members came from local, state, and national sportspeople groups and associations. The Wyoming Outfitters and Guides Association, NOLS, the Sublette County Outfitters and Guides Association Inc., and the Hoback Stock Association also joined this coalition.

In 2006 and 2007, CPWR, with the approval of Governor Freudenthal and the financial backing of Joe Ricketts, developed an extraordinary campaign to lobby all legislators in both Cheyenne and Washington DC, Senator Craig Thomas in particular. Outfitter-guides, along with ranchers from the area, volunteered to travel back and forth from the Hoback to Cheyenne and Washington to visit legislators. One of the outfitters working with CPWR was Dan Smitherman.

"I didn't come to Wyoming to be a tree hugger," Dan Smitherman stated. But he was one of the first big-game outfitters to identify the threat of energy development, and he became one of the leaders in the effort to save the Wyoming Range. A hunter and woodsman—tall and lean and dressed in black from hat to boots—he is striking looking, as well as articulate and forthright about his love of Wyoming.

Dan grew up in Alabama and, after graduating from high school, joined the Marine Corps during the Vietnam War. While he was in the service, one of the officers invited him to Wyoming for a pronghorn hunt. On that trip, Dan decided that this was the place he wanted to live. After his years with the marines, the Department of Defense hired him as an inspector of radar stations throughout the world, and there he met his wife, Sharon. Eventually he and Sharon resigned and came to Wyoming to make their home.

They settled in the Hoback Basin overlooking Bondurant. Dan became a big-game outfitter with a camp in the Wyoming Range, and Sharon went to work for the BTNF in Jackson. Dan spent months in the backcountry of the Wyoming Range, getting to know the country that was threatened by energy development.

"It's the locals' range," Dan told me when I interviewed him in August 2013. He described himself as a conservative voter who was in no way opposed to energy development. But like many others, he had seen the changes in the upper Green River Basin—the drop in wildlife populations—and could not bear the thought

FIGURE 50. Dan Smitherman, spokesperson for CPWR. Photo: Kelsey Dayton, courtesy of WyoFile.com.

of having the same thing happen in the area he knew and loved as a hunter and outfitter. He became active in opposing energy development in the Wyoming Range as both a member of CPWR and a concerned citizen and businessman.

"It made business sense to oppose these plans," Dan said. "Nobody's going to pay to recreate in an area crisscrossed with roads and big trucks roaring along them."

SENATOR CRAIG THOMAS entered the hospital with pneumonia just before the 2006 election. When he returned to work in early 2007—knowing he had leukemia—he began in earnest to draft two pieces of legislation: one to protect the Wyoming Range from future energy development, and the other to designate the Snake River headwaters as an integrated system of wild and scenic rivers. Thomas had been working for several years with American Rivers, GYC, and others to prepare the draft for this bill, which included the Hoback River and several tributaries.

In the spring of 2007, more than a year after the BTNF published its scoping letter on PXP's proposal for exploratory drilling, the forest service released a draft EIS (DEIS) for the Eagle Prospect project. It received more than nineteen thousand comments on the proposal.

Governor Freudenthal's letter of April 30, 2007 unequivocally opposed the project. He juxtaposed PXP's description of the three-well project as a "wildcatting expedition . . . in the off-chance hope of finding a little bit of gas" with company president Jim Flores's publicized remark about developing a nice field in the forest. The governor went on to point out that PXP "bolstered" Mr. Flores's public remarks in its filing with the U.S. Securities and Exchange Commission when it "equated the potential of this 'nice field' with the Jonah Field." He admitted his greater fear was "that history will view this project as the first domino that fell towards the industrialization of over 150,000 acres of oil and gas leases within the Wyoming Range. I will actively oppose any development scheme that will result in such an outcome."

The governor emphasized a range of possible alternatives and then listed his concerns about wildlife, long-term development, water, and socioeconomic factors that should be studied.[3] In addition to Governor Freudenthal's comments, the Wyoming Game and Fish Commission, the U.S. Department of the Interior, Wyoming Tourism, and the Jackson Hole Chamber of Commerce submitted statements, all opposing the development.

The conservation coalition worked with Dan Heilig, a legal consultant for Western Resources

Associates, who researched the entire leasing history of PXP and had a very comprehensive understanding of the process. According to Heilig, whom I interviewed in September 2013, the BTNF conducted its leasing and development procedures appropriately in the years following its forest plan publication: it determined availability and suitability of parts of the forest for leasing and conducted site-specific analyses to identify conditions requiring special stipulations.

Things began to break down after that. Between 1991, when the site-specific analyses were conducted for the watersheds involved in PXP's lease area, and 2007, when the DEIS was released, some important parts of the original environmental assessment fell through the cracks, including the Jackson Hole Stipulation.

According to Greg Clark, Big Piney district ranger who had overseen numerous exploratory wells in the past, most had proven unsuitable for development. He was quite certain that the same would be true of Eagle Prospect/Noble Basin. "It looked like a difficult and unproductive project," Greg told me in an interview in October 2013. He pointed out that there were no developed roads in the area, the winter snowpack would curtail year-round operations, and there was no adequate water source. He also noted that the gas-bearing formations in the Noble Basin were not as highly pressurized as those in the Pinedale Anticline, which would influence the amount of product recoverable and the ease with which it could be captured. "I never expected much to happen in that area," he said.

In 2006, when the DEIS was still being developed, Greg had taken PXP personnel on horseback to the area where they wanted to drill and pointed out the reasons it was not a good place for development. When the company remained serious about exploration, Greg encouraged PXP to submit a full-field development scenario. By this time, informal discussion between the

FIGURE 51. Governor Dave Fruedenthal *(right)* at a public meeting held by the BLM regarding energy development in the Pinedale Anticline. Photo courtesy of the BLM.

BTNF and PXP suggested that this plan would consist of seventeen pads and up to 136 gas wells. However, when the proposal arrived, it was for one well pad and up to three exploratory wells. The BTNF based its DEIS on that.

The coalition of conservation groups was ready to pounce when the DEIS appeared. In the introduction to their comments, the groups warned that "the choices the Forest Service makes today about whether to authorize further industrialization in one of our nation's most popular and ecologically important forests will chart a course that will either degrade or protect this invaluable public resource for generations."[4]

They detailed the many problems with the DEIS: it failed to consider a reasonable range of alternatives that included no action as required by NEPA and proposed instead only slight variations of one alternative. Although full-field development would be the reasonable result of successful exploratory drilling, it proposed only one well pad with up to three wells, consistent with an exploratory phase of development.

Wildlife resources, the coalition concluded, were given short shrift because the BTNF failed

FIGURE 52. Big Piney District Ranger Greg Clark, who over-saw much of the BTNF's work on energy development in the Wyoming Range. Photo: Susan Marsh.

to define suitable habitat and cumulative impact of the project on the Canada lynx and did not justify any adverse effects. The BTNF used outdated information on mule deer, which use the area during seasonal migration and parturition, and elk, which use it as a migratory route. And the BTNF did not incorporate information from Wyoming's wildlife experts on the impact on moose, which live in the area throughout the year.

The presumption in the DEIS that there was no impact on wildlife since affected big game could relocate to adjacent, unaffected habitats was counter to what had been proven scientifically. Choice of habitat by animals, the critique said, was not arbitrary but occurred because it best suited their needs to thrive and reproduce. As Aldo Leopold had pointed out, when animals are displaced from their prime habitat and have to occupy adjacent areas that are less suitable, survival and reproductive rates go down.

The conservation coalition noted that the DEIS did not discuss how stream habitat for native cutthroat trout would be maintained or improved as a result of the project. And the DEIS did not include monitoring indicator species

connected with wetland riparian, mountain meadow, and aspen habitats.

Further, the DEIS failed to provide adequate information about using and protecting ground and surface water that would be used in massive quantities during drilling. Nor did it adequately address ways to protect the air quality in Class I areas (wilderness and national parks), to control the myriad of pollutants used in drilling, or to prohibit flaring.

Last but not least, the conservationists noted that—according to a USFS directive—a district ranger should not be the official responsible for large, controversial projects like Eagle Prospect/ Noble Basin. In conclusion, the coalition stated, "The above-named conservation organizations request that the Forest Service suspend the Eagle Prospect/Noble Basin EIS until a full landscape analysis that addresses future oil and gas development is conducted for the Wyoming Range and the Bridger-Teton National Forest."[5]

Governor Freudenthal's comments—as well as those of state agencies, organizations, and individuals—convinced PXP to send a letter in June 2007 requesting the BTNF to withdraw the DEIS and formulate another document that considered a likely scenario for full-field development. Steven Rusch, vice president for environmental health, safety, and government affairs for the company, wrote that "PXP requests the Forest Service to take the unprecedented step to expand its current review to include an evaluation of impacts associated with development/ production from the PXP leases in the area of the Eagle Unit."[6]

Why PXP did not follow Greg Clark's advice to submit a proposal for full-field development, and why the BTNF accepted the company's proposal without the required full-field scenario, remain unanswered questions. As it happened, these and future delays in the NEPA analysis turned out to work in favor of the eventual buyout.

MORE COMMUNITIES OF PLANTS

In addition to open sagebrush steppe, aspen stands, and wetlands, specialized plant communities offer variety and beauty in the Hoback Basin.

Tall forb parks. "Tall forb" is a plant ecologist's term for the mixed herbaceous perennials that grow in deep, fine soils at elevations between 8,000 and 9,000 feet. The wildflowers of this ecotype leave pollen on the withers of a horse.

Some of the typical species in this plant community include fernleaf lovage, tall larkspur, sticky geranium, little sunflower, mule's ear, bracted lousewort, and lupine. Photo: Susan Marsh.

Conifer forest. Forested slopes comprise a relatively narrow band in the middle elevations between the steppe and mountain peaks. In many places, conifers mix with aspen stands and sagebrush as dictated by aspect, slope, and moisture.

The primary conifer species in midelevation forests include lodgepole pine, subalpine fir, and Engelmann spruce. Photo: Susan Marsh.

High mountains. The Hoback Basin is surrounded by peaks that climb more than 10,000 feet. Only the loftiest ramparts are part of the true alpine zone, where trees are reduced to wind-sculpted krummholz and wildflowers huddle low in the warming talus.

Snow lies late into July in the peaks surrounding the headwaters of Jamb Creek, where Peak 10,545 rises above the Highline Trail. Photo: Susan Marsh.

On December 13, 2007, the BTNF announced that it was reopening the public scoping period and that the environmental analysis would be expanded to address potential full-field development and a master development plan. "We are expanding the analysis because PXP's request for a full-field development alternative is a substantial change in the proposed action we analyzed in the original DEIS," Greg Clark wrote in a press release.[7] From that time forward, the proposed project was called the Eagle Prospect/Noble Basin Master Development Plan.

EARLIER THAT YEAR, spirits were lifted by the news that Senator Thomas had announced his intention to introduce federal legislation to protect the Wyoming Range from further mineral leasing. His staff had been working with the BTNF for the previous months on the Wyoming Range Legacy Act (WRLA) and Snake Headwaters Legacy Act. The first drafts of both bills were completed in May 2007. But that fall, the entire community was shocked and saddened when Senator Thomas died of leukemia. All who knew him thought he was an outstanding legislator and a genuinely sincere and dedicated public servant. At his memorial service, Senator Michael Enzi read from Tom Reed's book, *Give Me Mountains for My Horses*.

During deliberations to fill the empty senate seat, Governor Freudenthal made it clear that he expected Senator Thomas's successor to implement the draft legislation. He then announced his choice: John Barrasso. All who had worked with Senator Thomas hoped that Barrasso, with the help of Senator Enzi, would continue Thomas's commitment to protect the Wyoming Range.

In October 2008, Senator Barrasso introduced the WRLA, along with the Snake Headwaters Legacy Act. It became part of wider-reaching legislation, the Omnibus Public Land Management Act, signed into law by President Barack Obama in March 2009. The coalitions, as well as the citizens of Wyoming, are deeply grateful to Senators Barrasso and Enzi—both conservative Republicans as was their late colleague—for this outstanding conservation accomplishment. In addition to protecting 1.2 million acres of pristine land from mineral leasing, the WRLA made provisions to allow existing leases covering about 70,000 acres to be donated, purchased, or traded so they could be legally and permanently retired.

The WRLA did not affect the contested 44,720 acres but left the fate of these leases in the hands of the BTNF after it had completed a new environmental analysis. In the spring of 2008, the BTNF had announced its intention to prepare a DEIS for the 44,720 acres.

The WRLA was a game changer: by ensuring that any relinquished leases within the legislative boundary could never be re-leased, the law held the key to a new possibility: preventing development of the Eagle Prospect/Noble Basin project. With this guarantee, a buyout would attract donors.

While it was not the first withdrawal of public lands from energy development, the WRLA's profound importance cannot be underestimated. Precedents existed: disputes in Montana on the Front Range of the Rocky Mountains had been settled by withdrawing more than 100,000 acres within the Lewis and Clark National Forest, and a similar dispute in New Mexico had resulted in preserving 45,000 acres of public land. But the magnitude of withdrawing 1.2 million acres was unprecedented in the annals of United States land policy.

The significance of the legislation reverberated through the entire community and the coalitions whose members had been proactively lobbying for legislative action. The WRLA influenced the relationship between corporate interests and public lands. It reinforced the importance of public participation in national and local governmental land

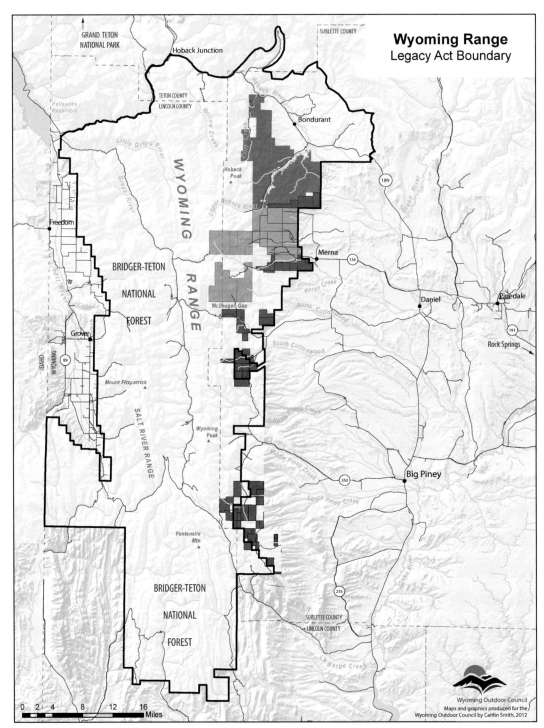

MAP 9. The area protected by Senator Barrasso's 2009 Wyoming Range Legacy Act. More than 1.2 million acres was included in the legislation that was signed into law. Map by Caitlin Smith, courtesy of the Wyoming Outdoor Council.

FIGURE 53. View of Hoback Peak from the Wyoming Range National Recreation Trail. This is part of the area protected by the Wyoming Range Legacy Act. Photo: Susan Marsh.

policies. At the local level, it united people with divergent political and ideological perspectives who had worked both together and separately toward a common goal. Appropriately, it was an excellent example of bipartisan cooperation and proved that conservation is not a one-sided issue.

Accompanying the WRLA was the passage of the Snake Headwaters Legacy Act, later renamed the Craig Thomas Snake Headwaters Legacy Act to honor its creator. The legislation was designed to protect the major streams of an entire watershed, that of the upper Snake River in Wyoming. It included rivers within the BTNF and Yellowstone and Grand Teton National Parks.

American Rivers was one of the first groups to work with Senator Thomas on this act. In September of 2003, Scott Bosse began work for GYC, serving on a steering committee to launch a campaign to protect the headwaters of the Snake River and its tributaries that were eligible for wild and scenic river status. By 2009, he was employed by American Rivers. His involvement in river protection and his friendship with Thomas, as well as the prominent status of American Rivers, contributed greatly to the ultimate success of the coalition of conservation groups.

During the years when Scott Bosse and others worked toward a wild and scenic river designation

FIGURE 54. Scott Bosse, whose work with the Greater Yellowstone Coalition and American Rivers helped raise awareness of the unique beauty of the Wyoming Range, including its spectacular streams. Photo courtesy of American Rivers/ Scotte Bosse.

for the Snake River and its tributaries, Senator Thomas's Washington staff worked with the USFS's national rivers liaison, Jackie Deidrich, as well as BTNF staff, which provided information about eligible wild and scenic rivers. The BTNF inventory of eligible rivers became the basis for the initial bill. During its development, Senator Thomas (and, later, Senator Barrasso) worked with local governments and state agencies. The BTNF inventory included twenty-four eligible rivers and nearly five hundred river miles within the Snake River watershed. Opposition to any river designation in Sublette and Lincoln Counties resulted in reducing the mileage in the final bill since the congressional delegation was attempting to satisfy everyone, including those who saw river designation as a threat. In the end, thirteen river segments within the BTNF were included in the legislation—mostly within Teton County—making it the leading county in the nation for wild and scenic river miles (it also contains designated rivers within Yellowstone and Grand Teton National Parks).

IN AUGUST 2009, many of the persons who had taken part in the passage of the WRLA met at Gary Amerine's outfitter camp on the Greys River to celebrate the occasion. Gary later described the way all the forces seemed to come together to accomplish this great achievement as "a perfect storm." The BTNF DEIS for the PXP project seemed to be indefinitely stalled: since the first DEIS was published in April 2007 and later withdrawn, the target date for releasing the new document had been delayed numerous times, and more than two years had passed. The people who gathered at Gary's camp that August afternoon set aside their frustrations over this delay to celebrate the passage of the WRLA and the Craig Thomas Snake Headwaters Legacy Act.

One person not present to celebrate the day was game warden Duane Hyde, who had played a significant role in protecting the Wyoming Range. Unfortunately, like Senator Thomas, he had died. He was a Star Valley rancher on the western front of the Salt River Range and was the first hired game warden in Wyoming.

"Duane was instrumental in this," Tom Reed told me in our March 2014 interview. "He was the face of the WRLA. He was the most senior game warden in the state of Wyoming when he retired. He had badge number one. He was a very good friend of mine, and he was an outspoken guy in favor of the WRLA."

Many men and women like him—too numerous to mention here—also contributed significantly to the successful passage of these laws. It was a community, regional, and national effort.

During the celebration, BLM officials announced that the agency would not accept pending bids on twenty-three oil and gas lease parcels totaling 23,757 acres in the new Wyoming Range withdrawal area. The BLM had determined not to issue the leases in light of the WRLA and a preliminary IBLA ruling.

In a moving statement delivered to those assembled, Tom Reed described the deep feelings among the people of this "homegrown, grassroots movement" who use the Wyoming Range for hunting, fishing, hiking, or just basking in its pristine ambience:

> It's that feeling you get when you're standing on the creek in the middle of the Wyoming Range, and you are totally zoned in on what you are doing, and you catch a Snake River cutthroat. It is the pure genetic strain of fish that swam in those waters five thousand years ago. And then you drive up over the road a little and then down into the head of La Barge and catch another subspecies that is also the pure strain of that primal fish. If you drive a little farther and on to Smith's Fork, if you're lucky you might catch another subspecies of cutthroat trout! All of these species are 99 percent pure stock that swam in those waters five thousand years ago. The question is why would anyone want to destroy such a habitat that connects the people and animals to thousands of years of habitation in the Wyoming Range? No other range in the United States can proclaim such an evolution, and for this reason alone—for its actual genetic connection to the past—the Wyoming Range was a valid candidate for withdrawal and protection from the destruction of industrialization.

The WRLA was the ballast that kept the campaigns of outfitters, sportspeople, and conservationists afloat for the journey ahead. In their own way, they had all done the kind of "good work" that E. F. Schumacher described in his unforgettable book *Small Is Beautiful*, the kind of work that leads to a better and more ecologically sustainable planet.

The coalitions are classic examples of the way well-planned grassroots organizations, made up of the people living in the area, whose livelihood depends on these lands, can successfully ward off industrialization. Such lands may contain some wilderness or roadless areas that are wild and untrammeled, as well as ecosystems that—though used—remain healthy and balanced. Such places can be enjoyed in many ways by many creatures, including humans. They can be fawning areas for mule deer; summer ranges and migratory areas for deer, elk, moose, and pronghorn; and habitat for many more of those "others" that share this earth with us, from trout to sparrows to grizzly bears.

These lands can concurrently serve humans as accessible areas for family camping, summer grazing for ranchers' cattle and sheep, hunting grounds and fishing streams for outfitters and guides, and a gamut of recreational uses—from hunting and fishing to hiking and photography. All of these stakeholders—to use the jargon of the day—can thoughtfully and carefully share a place like this without doing harm, thus maintaining its ecological integrity.

The basic principle of multiple use states that although one activity may be dominant in an area, it should not degrade the ecology, rendering it no longer useful for other purposes in the future. For this reason, oil and gas development and industrialization, as it is typically conducted, make multiple use impossible. They alter the land and make it unsuitable for other uses. This is why energy development must be cautiously contained and greatly restricted in the remaining intact ecosystems, where aesthetic and spiritual values are more important to the public than economic profit.

WHEN THE WRLA was signed, the primary objective of CPWR had been accomplished, and the

FIGURES 55A AND B.
Celebration at Gary Amerine's outfitting camp on Greys River in August 2009. Senator Barrasso and Governor Freudenthal joined several hundred others to mark passage of the Wyoming Range Legacy Act and the Craig Thomas Snake Headwaters Legacy Act. Photos: Susan Marsh.

group became inactive. While all interested parties awaited release of the updated DEIS for PXP's Eagle Prospect/Noble Basin project, a small committee formed to negotiate with PXP, hoping to reach an agreement on drilling practices and mitigation. Convinced that the PXP project would happen in spite of the WRLA, they sought ways to minimize the effects of inevitable development.

Among those negotiating were Gary Amerine, representing the Wyoming Outfitters and Guides Association; Joe Ricketts, who had funded much of the WRLA lobbying; and others not previously

FIGURE 56. The Red Castles on the east slope of the Wyoming Range. Deep red strata contrast with the bright green of an aspen stand, regenerated after a 1940 wildfire. Photo: Susan Marsh.

recognized as involved—Sublette County Outfitters and Guides Association Inc., the Hoback Stock Association, and the Wyoming chapter of Sportsmen for Fish and Wildlife. And throughout deliberations, Governor Freudenthal supported their efforts to come to an acceptable agreement with PXP on development.

"I did not want them to drill, but I wanted to be a part of it if they did," Gary Amerine told me in our October 2013 interview. "I wanted some

oversight." He praised the PXP representatives he met: "They were very concerned about doing it right. Very concerned. A lot of people don't believe that, but I do. I would never have dealt with them otherwise."

TWS and the WOC continued to disagree with this approach. Dan Smitherman, who had been active in the CPWR from its beginning, realized the limits of negotiation. He decided that any development of the leases, no matter how

FIGURE 57. Home-page banner on CFWR's website, the organization that worked from 2010 to 2013 to consummate a buyout of PXP's energy leases. Courtesy of Citizens for the Wyoming Range.

carefully carried out, would devastate the Noble Basin, so he turned his efforts to preserving the land he loved, not mitigating the damage that would surely occur.

Understanding the importance of an active citizen organization, the conservation coalition agreed that an effective spokesperson was essential to interact with the community. With the CPWR refusing to challenge PXP's right to develop its leases, they began talking with Dan about leading the citizen's organization under a slightly different name: Citizens for the Wyoming Range (CFWR).

Dan was a good choice, a person who was trusted and could relate to local citizens. It was astute of Steff Kessler and Lisa McGee to invite him to join their efforts to preserve the Wyoming Range. This trio—working together as they did— were in large part responsible for the eventual retirement of the PXP leases. They provide an excellent example of collaboration based on a mix of skills and strengths. Steff was a natural leader with political know-how; Dan was a trusted voice in the community; Lisa contributed a sharp focus on important legal details that were missing from

environmental documents. Without these exceptional people—working for three different NGOs (TWS, CFWR, and WOC), I might be looking at gas field support trucks going up and down the Hoback road today.

Steff, Dan, and Lisa saw the summer of 2010 as a crucial period when a coordinated effort to stop the development of the leases was no longer an impossible dream. Armed with the WRLA and its provisions that ensured leases voluntarily donated or sold could never be leased again, they felt new hope that drilling in the Hoback Basin could be stopped.

In mid-July, I attended a meeting at the home of Dan and Yvonne Bailey on the upper Hoback River, sponsored by TWS. Steff Kessler and Diane Corsick of TWS showed maps of the planned drilling site and laid out plans for responding to the DEIS when it was finally published. Many in the group still questioned whether the PXP project could be stopped, believing they should wait for the DEIS and then work to minimize the project's impact. I agreed with those who felt that our major effort should be directed at stopping the drilling and insisting on an alternative in the

DEIS that would retire the leases. At this meeting, Steff introduced Dan and Sharon Smitherman.

In early August, Steff announced the formation of CFWR with Dan Smitherman as its spokesperson. As they awaited the publication of the new DEIS, the conservation coalition orchestrated an ambitious series of events. They scheduled four community outreach meetings in Jackson, Pinedale, Bondurant, and Hoback Ranches; two public hikes to the drilling sites that attracted more than fifty people; two overflights of the area and the Pinedale Anticline for media and officials; and a horseback ride to the proposed site with officials from the governor's office, the Wyoming Game and Fish Department, the EPA, and Senator Barrasso's office. There was also a special horseback ride into the area for USFS officials, including the BTNF acting forest supervisor, deputy forest supervisor, and the regional forester based in Ogden, Utah.

Lloyd Dorsey of GYC joined one of the groups hiking into the Noble Basin. He had recently written a study on the value of wildlife in the Wyoming Range; hunting in Noble Basin and the surrounding area generates about two million dollars for the local economy. He emphasized that the area is critical habitat for lynx and other animals besides big game. "This is a connector between three or four mountain ranges," Dorsey told the group on the Noble Basin field trip. "This is a wildlife crossroads. You've got lynx and black bear coming through here, as well as hoofed animals. . . . Let's see if there's a trade out or a buyout," Dorsey added. "I think this is a prime candidate."[8] This was the first mention in public of a possible buyout. In the following meetings, the emphasis shifted to retiring the leases, rather than trying to minimize the impact of drilling.

Through the summer and fall, CFWR and other environmental NGOs continued outreach to local citizens. As a contingency measure—in case the efforts to stop the drilling failed—they

encouraged the public to exert pressure on the BTNF to require maximum environmental protection and mitigation so costly that PXP would find it unprofitable to develop their leases. As part of this effort, they developed a working document that they called a "gold standard" of restrictions and practices if development took place.

SDSBT held a meeting to prepare to respond to the DEIS. TWS and CFWR sponsored meetings throughout Wyoming to raise awareness about a possible buyout. In Rock Springs—a town dependent on mineral resources—more than sixty people packed into the library auditorium. Participants acknowledged the appropriateness of oil and gas development in some areas but voiced their fears about loss of access and wildlife, as well as water contamination and air pollution. Some places, they said, just shouldn't be developed.

Mike Burd, a resident of Green River, had guided local reporters during overflights in a light plane supported by EcoFlight, a nonprofit organization. "They [PXP] have long-term plans to make the Jonah Field of the woods," he told me on the phone in September 2013. "These people are from Houston, and they don't care about Wyoming. They care about what's in the ground."

Dan Smitherman made continual entries on the CFWR listserv to make everyone aware of developments. In November, the Jackson Hole Conservation Alliance hosted two meetings where Dan and Lisa McGee updated audiences on the status of the PXP project and answered questions. And on November 29, 2010, CFWR invited Gloria Flora, founder of Sustainable Obtainable Solutions, to talk in Jackson about her experiences as forest supervisor at the Lewis and Clark National Forest in Montana. This meeting was planned around the expected release of the BTNF's revised DEIS; however, the document was still not ready for public review by the end of November. Another change in key BTNF personnel had occurred in 2010: Greg Clark had retired in

FIGURE 58. Hunters packing into the Grayback Roadless Area, which comprises more than 315,000 acres of backcountry in the northern Wyoming Range. Photo: Susan Marsh.

January, and Kniffy Hamilton in May. Jacqueline Buchanan, the newly named forest supervisor, had started work just before this meeting.

Flora encouraged the standing-room-only crowd by affirming that their hope to prevent development was not an impossible dream. As supervisor of the Lewis and Clark National Forest, she had decided to put the Rocky Mountain Front off-limits to oil and gas leasing for a period of ten to fifteen years. The U.S. Congress later withdrew the 100,000-acre area from further leasing.

Flora emphasized the importance of citizen participation in her project, which was very similar to the struggle for Hoback Basin. Her thoughts appeared later in an essay in the anthology *The Energy Reader:*

Far-sighted people had already been pressing for protection for the Front for years

before I showed up. Their steadfast defense of the land and its inhabitants, including the winged, the finned, and the four-legged, was truly remarkable. They proved to me again and again that it's not the commodities that come from public lands that make the difference in the quality of our lives; it's the experience and memories, the sum of our relationship with the land we love that make us better human beings. Our legacy of wild landscapes is worth far more than anything money can buy.[9]

Flora inspired the crowd to pursue all options to prevent energy development in the Hoback Basin, and while many expressed skepticism before the meeting, most were more optimistic after it. If she and others had made it work for the Rocky Mountain Front Range in Montana, they could do the same for the Hoback.

136 natural gas wells coming to the Bridger-Teton National Forest

A drilling proposal on the Bridger-Teton is the problem.
Lessons from Montana might point to a solution.

Citizens for the Wyoming Range

welcomes **Gloria Flora**, former forest supervisor and now an advocate for wild places, who will share success stories from Montana's Rocky Mountain Front.

Oil and gas companies agreed to voluntarily relinquish their leases on the Front, recognizing some places are too special to drill.

Come join us for a discussion about how lessons from Montana could provide solutions for safeguarding the Upper Hoback.

Monday, Nov. 29, 6 p.m.
St. John's Episcopal Church
145 N. Cache
Jackson
For more info:
(307) 690-1737 www.wyomingrange.org

CITIZENS
for the
WYOMING RANGE

PRSRT STD
US POSTAGE PAID
PERMIT # 81
JACKSON, WY

FIGURE 59. The front and back of a flier announcing the November 2010 public meeting sponsored by CFWR where Gloria Floria spoke. Courtesy of Citizens for the Wyoming Range.

WHEN TOM REED of TU began working with CPWR, one of his major goals was to negotiate an agreement with PXP to ensure environmental protection and mitigation of harmful effects when it developed its leases. As part of that agreement, PXP offered to relinquish 28,000 of its 63,550 acres of leases, most of them in isolated parcels unconnected to the Eagle Prospect/Noble Basin area but still in important backcountry areas in or near the Wyoming Range.

After passage of the WRLA and talking with PXP for three years, the parties involved were anxious to finalize this agreement. However, Tom Reed was not ready to sign off. From TU's point of view, the agreement did not offer enough protection for fisheries, wildlife, or people in the Hoback Basin.

Apparently other members of the negotiating team felt it was best to proceed without the signatures of several participants, including TU. Neither Joe Ricketts nor the state of Wyoming signed the final agreement. In the end, just two parties involved in the negotiation—the Wyoming chapter of Sportsmen for Fish and Wildlife, represented by Bob Wharff, and the Sublette County Outfitters and Guides Association Inc., represented by Gary Amerine, signed and submitted to the BTNF a document titled "Term Sheet: Wyoming Range Conservation & Noble Basin Development Agreement."

It is not clear exactly why some members of the original negotiating group were not included when this document was finally signed. Each person we interviewed had a slightly different take on what happened and why. It does seem clear that it was a good effort undertaken by people who understood PXP's right to develop its leases and who wanted to influence the way development took place. Gary Amerine felt that the effort produced true gains for environmental conservation: "We got 28,000 acres donated at no cost, the most sensitive part of the area, Cliff Creek, $5 million dollars in Game and Fish [Department] money, and $1.1 million on water mitigation," he told me in our 2013 interview.

Tom Reed agreed. "It was fantastic what PXP had agreed to for Cliff Creek, which is a huge spawning and summer habitat," he said on the phone in 2014.

On December 10, 2010, the parties that signed the term sheet announced that a coalition of outfitters and sportspeople had reached a sweeping agreement to preserve the Wyoming Range and contain oil and gas drilling. The announcement described the history of the term sheet that had been submitted to the BTNF.

It stated that Kevin Campbell, president of the Hoback Stock Association, and Terry Pollard of the Sublette County Outfitters and Guides Association, had signed the agreement but did not mention the state of Wyoming, TU, or Joe Ricketts, who had been involved earlier in the negotiations with PXP.

The term sheet proposed sixteen conditions agreed upon by PXP, "contingent upon the enactment of a Record of Decision by the USFS that does not create unreasonable barriers to pursue development of oil and gas development in the project area."[10]

Members of the conservation coalition believed that the term sheet offered little more than off-site mitigation and restrictions that would have been required regardless. Many questioned the way the negotiations had taken place: in private, without including other interested parties. "It's a proposal, not a deal," one reporter observed.[11]

In a letter to the BTNF regarding the term sheet, CFWR and other conservation groups stated,

> PXP has offered some important concessions, not the least of which is the permanent retirement of its valid oil and gas leases on 28,000 acres of national forest land in the Cliff Creek area. We applaud PXP for contemplating actions that further the long-term conservation of the Bridger-Teton. This welcomed announcement, however, comes at too high a price and with substantial strings attached.[12]

On December 10, 2010—the same day that the term sheet was made public—the BTNF, after years of delay, finally released the DEIS for the Eagle Prospect/Noble Basin Master Development Plan, intended to replace the 2007 document. Although the updated DEIS did include a

OUR forest on OUR terms.

The Upper Hoback Basin in the rugged Wyoming Range of western Wyoming provides critical habitat and a vital crossroads for migrating wildlife in the Yellowstone ecosystem. It is a treasured hunting ground and recreational area for generations of Wyoming families. It sits in the pristine headwaters of the Wild and Scenic Hoback River.

Home to moose, deer, elk, pronghorn, native trout and the elusive Canada lynx, this remote corner of the Bridger-Teton is now threatened by Plains Exploration & Production Company's (PXP) proposal to site a full-field natural gas development. PXP wants to drill 136 wells on 17 well pads and build 30 miles of industrial roads, man-camps, compressor stations, pipelines, waste treatment plants and more.

DIDN'T THE WYOMING RANGE LEGACY ACT OF 2009 PROTECT THIS PART OF THE FOREST FROM OIL AND GAS DEVELOPMENT?

The Legacy Act prohibits future leasing, but does not affect the pre-existing leases held by PXP. We know the only way to avoid destroying the Upper Hoback is to avoid development altogether in this very special place. The crux, unfortunately, is that the Forest Service cannot easily deny development once leases have been issued. Because PXP has valid leases, the best way to protect the Hoback is to convince the company to agree to donate or sell these leases. And because all of PXP's leases are within the protected boundary of the Wyoming Range Legacy Act, once retired, the area can never be leased again.

This is not without precedent. Oil and gas companies have sold or donated hundreds of thousands of acres of oil and gas leases to protect forest lands in Montana, and Wyoming deserves this same win-win solution.

WE NEED YOUR HELP TO SAVE THE HOBACK:
BUY-OUT OR NOT, WE STILL NEED PUBLIC COMMENTS

The Forest Service cannot force PXP to accept a buy-out. So in case a deal cannot be reached, we must tell the Forest Service to do its job right. The wildlife, waters, air quality, hunting and recreational uses of the Upper Hoback must be protected if this project moves forward. The Bridger-Teton National Forest is soliciting your feedback on its Draft Environmental Impact Statement (DEIS) about PXP's plan. Make your voice heard during the public comment period. **The deadline for comments is March 11th.**

PRODUCED BY CITIZENS FOR THE WYOMING RANGE ~ WWW.WYOMINGRANGE.ORG
PO BOX 349, BONDURANT, WY 82922 ▲ (307) 690-1737 ▲ DAN@WYOMINGRANGE.ORG

FIGURE 60. The flier produced by CFWR reminding people to comment on the draft EIS for the Eagle Prospect/Noble Basin project. Courtesy of Citizens for the Wyoming Range.

development scenario as required, conservation groups and sportspeople alike were discouraged, especially since the BTNF had promised to develop alternatives that met all of the provisions required by the forest plan.

"I'm somewhat disappointed," Dan Smitherman noted, "particularly in the area of wildlife.

I didn't see any substantial difference from what was originally proposed."[13]

Although the DEIS failed to meet everyone's hopes and expectations, members of the public were well-organized and ready with pen or computer at hand to respond before the due date for comments, March 10, 2011.

6

Too Special to Drill
(2010–2013)

U PON PUBLICATION OF THE DEIS FOR THE
Eagle Prospect/Noble Basin Master Development Plan, advocates from throughout the
nation joined forces with locals to submit their
comments by the deadline. The conservation
coalition had prepared well for this moment.
During the summer, Linda Cooper had met with
SDSBT members to make plans for collaboratively
reviewing the DEIS and submitting appropriate
comments individually. Linda also planned to
submit comments that represented the collective
sentiments and insights of SDSBT members.

CFWR, under the leadership of Dan Smitherman, Steff Kessler, and Lisa McGee, met weekly
with a small group to plan strategies, share ideas,
inform the public, and keep the momentum going
during the review period. They also held monthly
conference calls with a larger group to answer
questions and keep everyone informed of developments. CFWR's goal was to include all interested participants in a community-based effort.

Dan Smitherman sent a reminder to the
members of CFWR that the DEIS was available for

review. He suggested in the e-mail that we attend
one of the three public information meetings
scheduled in January 2011 in Jackson, Bondurant,
and Pinedale. His message clearly set out the
expectations of CFWR:

> Citizens for the Wyoming Range is not
> opposed to energy development, and we
> understand that PXP has a legal right to make
> its proposal, but we believe that responsible
> drilling means that some places are too spe-
> cial to drill. We think the Upper Hoback is one
> of those special places. Congress recognized
> this when it passed the Wyoming Range Leg-
> acy Act and withdrew these lands from future
> oil and gas leasing. The Legacy Act created a
> market-based solution for existing leases, and
> we urge PXP to sell and retire its leases in the
> spirit of the legislation.
>
> Although we don't believe a full field
> industrial gas field in this special place can
> ever be fully mitigated, if PXP chooses not to
> negotiate a buy-out, then the Forest Service

FIGURE 61. Beaver ponds provide habitat for a number of wildlife species, from native fish and amphibians to songbirds, raptors, and moose. Photo: Susan Marsh.

must require the very toughest standards to ensure air and water quality, wildlife and backcountry values are safeguarded. Our forest deserves nothing less.

Our health and mountain vistas deserve better, our safety and pure waters deserve better, and our wildlife and hunting traditions deserve better. This is the public's forest—and PXP must respect our terms. Our forests deserve the best.[1]

An accounting of the economic value of wildlife in the Hoback Basin and the proposed PXP drilling area by Lloyd Dorsey for GYC contained many important facts and figures. This document was a valuable reference for those writing comments. Lloyd showed that big-game and trophy hunters alone brought revenue estimated at more

than two million dollars to the state each year.[2] That figure did not include the amount brought in by anglers and vacationers.

The report referenced two desired future conditions (DFCs) from the BTNF forest plan of 1990 with a wildlife focus. DFC 10 included the statement that "all surface-disturbing activities are designed to have no effect or beneficial effects on wildlife."[3] DFC 12 was described as "an area managed for high-quality wildlife habitat and escape cover, big-game hunting opportunities, and dispersed recreation activities."[4]

Lloyd's report pointed out that the "importance of this area for wildlife habitat has actually increased over the years due to the fragmentation of the landscape by increased oil and gas development throughout the Green River Basin." He then went on to list the great diversity of creatures that use the contested area, including cutthroat trout, migratory songbirds, raptors, sage grouse, Canada lynx, and big game.[5]

Lloyd's valuation highlighted the great natural treasure that Eagle Prospect/Noble Basin was: a long-standing ecosystem that remained viable and healthy, providing habitat for all creatures; an ecological asset that could not be counted in dollars and cents. Susan and I believe that these creatures and their habitat are priceless; they cannot be reproduced or replaced.

DURING THE COMMENT period, Lisa McGee, Steff Kessler, and Dan Heilig researched and published an in-depth response to PXP's statement that "any drilling proposed for the Eagle Prospect/Noble Basin area would meet a gold standard for resource protection." They decided to document what a gold standard would look like, including best practices to minimize the impact of mineral exploration and development in the Hoback Basin. Drawing heavily from practices and requirements already in use in the BLM's Jonah and Pinedale Anticline gas fields, they included conservation goals, mitigation, and the policies and procedures, rules and regulations established by state and federal agencies. They emphasized the need to protect not only land-based resources but also air and water quality and public health.

They began with a disclaimer that the "Hoback Basin in the Bridger-Teton National Forest is not an appropriate place to locate an industrial gas field." They held PXP accountable for its public commitments and set out a defensible gold standard with conservation goals that companies planning energy development on public lands should follow to achieve the highest environmental safeguards. Topics covered included consistency with forest plans; reclamation; the importance of bonds (a sufficient amount to fully reclaim disturbed areas and restore any lands or surface water damaged by drilling); prevention of pollution;

FIGURE 62. Two fishermen take a young man out for his first fly-casting lesson at the confluence of Dell Creek and the Hoback River. Photo: Susan Marsh.

providing public safety and information; protection of wildlife, watersheds, water resources, and water quality; steep slopes and unstable soil; air quality and related air issues; and inventoried roadless areas and potential wildernesses.

Later, Lisa expressed her concern about this effort: "I often said the worst-case scenario is that we'd have the most highly regulated gas field in Wyoming (assuming they met the gold standard criteria), but the best-case scenario would be that PXP could not, in fact, meet this standard and the project would prove to be uneconomical, leading them to negotiate a sale of their leases."[6]

It should be emphasized that the gold standard document is a compilation of forest plan standards, best management practices, and other

THE WYOMING RANGE AND UPPER GREEN RIVER BASIN

The Hoback Basin is part of a larger landscape that includes the Gros Ventre and Wyoming Ranges, the adjacent upper Green River, Hoback Canyon downstream, and even Jackson Hole, where deer and pronghorn migrate for the summer.

The western portal of Hoback Canyon between the Gros Ventre Range and Beaver Mountain. Photo: Susan Marsh

criteria commonly used by federal agencies. The standard realistically states what is necessary to protect the environment and is not a strategy to make the project unprofitable. On the contrary, if gold-standard protections are enacted well before drilling or other development takes place, companies learn what the project will cost them. In some cases, the cost may be prohibitive. In cases where the product is valuable, high-cost development may be worth it to the company.

Insisting on strict stipulations might make development unprofitable, and the conservation coalition made no secret that it hoped that would be the case. However, the gold standard was more than political hardball—it asked the BTNF to do what it was supposed to do.

During the comment period, many letters to the editor appeared in regional newspapers. Among them was a "Guest Shot" column published in the *Jackson Hole News & Guide* and written by Gregg Sherrill, CEO of Tenneco, Inc. He wrote about his ties with the energy industry and his support of development in general. "I also believe that development should be considered and balanced, with provisions made for special and unique circumstances," he wrote. "These circumstances can at times be influenced by economics and at others by something less tangible but no less real. America is a beautiful country. We see daily evidence of that beauty in those special places like the Upper Hoback." He encouraged readers to write to the Forest Service and express their commitment to the Wyoming Range.[7]

By the end of the ninety-day comment period, the BTNF had received nearly sixty thousand comments on the PXP Eagle Prospect/ Noble Basin Master Development Plan, most of them opposing development. Among them was a response from newly elected governor Matt Mead, who had taken office in January 2011. He stated that the DEIS lacked data and could result in unacceptable impacts to wildlife and air

and water quality. "The Forest Service must fully consider all the probable impacts to all major game species, including elk, moose, mule deer and pronghorn," Mead wrote. He continued,

Baseline data must be established and serve to outline the short- and long-term impacts that this project will have on an area that serves as crucial winter range for elk and moose, and seasonal and transitional habitat for mule deer and pronghorn.

The Wyoming Game and Fish Department has articulated its concerns related to water quality and quantity, erosion, monitoring, buffers, road development and maintenance, and other associated impacts to fisheries. All these concerns must be considered, addressed in full and incorporated into the final EIS.

In sum, adequate baseline data regarding wildlife, air quality and water quality is needed as well as a comprehensive plan developed by the Forest Service, together with stakeholders, for siting, development, monitoring, production, and reclamation.[8]

Primary concerns expressed in response to the 2007 DEIS were still not entirely addressed in the 2010 document. Wildlife and air quality remained major concerns, as did groundwater quality. The 2010 DEIS, while referring to some things covered in the 1990 forest plan, did not include required stipulations for energy leasing and misrepresented that plan's open-road density standards. Maps in the DEIS did not show inventoried roadless areas, that part of the forest subject to stipulations in the 1947 Krug Memorandum, or locations of steep slopes and unstable soils requiring a no-surface-occupancy stipulation. The same maps did show roads and other facilities proposed for these areas.

Respondents wondered whether the BTNF would use the information from their comments

FIGURE 63. Mount Darby overlooks a series of beaver ponds along Coal Creek. Much of the forest in this scene has since burned. Photo: Susan Marsh.

to formulate a plan that looked substantially different from the document they were reviewing. The focus in general was to convince the BTNF to write a supplemental DEIS that would remedy the deficiencies and acknowledge respondents' comments. Perhaps, it was hoped, the third time would hold the charm.

THE YEARS 2010 and 2011 were busy ones for the BTNF oil and gas leasing program. While working on the analysis for the Eagle Prospect/Noble Basin Master Development Plan, the BTNF also

attempted to complete its analysis of proposed leasing of 44,720 acres on the east slope of the Wyoming Range, which it had begun in the spring of 2008. After WOC discovered that Stanley Energy, one of the companies with an interest in these leases, was paying for the environmental analysis, critics feared a conflict of interest. In its comments about the 2008 scoping notice, TU stated that there was a "disturbing relationship between the Forest Service and Stanley Energy that necessitates the Forest Service halt the ongoing process and reassess and reorganize the system to allow for public involvement." Governor Fruedenthal likewise objected to ". . . allowing Stanley Energy undue influence during the development of an environmental study to determine whether to allow oil and gas drilling on the Wyoming Range land."[9]

The BTNF acknowledged that "mistakes were made" and went back to the drawing board to prepare the draft supplemental EIS for the 44,720 acres, using its staff instead of a third-party contractor.

Mike Burd, a member of United Steel Workers of America Local 13214, which represents hundreds of workers at southwestern Wyoming trona mines and soda-ash plants, was quoted in a CFWR news release, saying that if the leases were validated, it would spark an even bigger battle than the Eagle Prospect/Noble Basin project.

"Our members fish and hunt in these areas even more than the Hoback, so we are watching this one closely," he said. Burd said the original proposal for leasing in the Wyoming Range in 2005 had caused the Wyoming AFL-CIO to issue its first formal leasing protest in the history of the organization. "We are an extraction state, but there are places we don't want to drill because of our Wyoming way of life and what we like to do," he said. "That's what got us all together to pass the Wyoming Range Legacy Act, and it's what will get these last leases cancelled for good."[10]

When the DEIS for the 44,720 acres was released in January 2010, Forest Supervisor Kniffy Hamilton proposed to suspend or cancel contested leases as part of the preferred alternative. "The no-leasing alternative avoids impacts to the Canada lynx and precludes cumulative impacts to air quality and mule deer,"[11] she said.

Hamilton retired in May 2010. The final supplemental DEIS was completed at the end of 2010. Hamilton's successor, Jacqueline Buchanan, signed the record of decision on January 25, 2011, and notified the public that she had decided to

follow Hamilton's lead, selecting Alternative 1, the no-action alternative. The "Purpose and Need" section of the final supplemental EIS prominently headlined a reasonably foreseeable development scenario with this introduction: "It is the operational and development activities that occur after a lease is issued that can have environmental, social and economic impacts. To assess these potential effects, it is necessary to project the type and amount of activity that is reasonably foreseeable as a consequence of authorizing the BLM to lease these lands."[12]

These were words that many members of the public had been waiting to read, for some USFS officials had downplayed the significance of decisions to lease, using such statements to the media as "the act of leasing does not result in surface disturbance."

Supervisor Buchanan stated that she was "not authorizing the Bureau of Land Management to offer 35 lease parcels located within the Wyoming Range and totaling 44,720 acres, at this time." She explained that her decision was based on "the sensitivity and values of the area, the magnitude of other activities currently underway or planned with potentially cumulative impacts, and the concerns of citizens, organizations, and other agencies."[13]

She supported her decision in several ways. One was the continuous and rapid expansion of energy development in the Green River Basin, far beyond what the NEPA process had analyzed and approved. Originally authorized wells in the Jonah Field had increased from 450 to 3,100 through an in-fill process that designated more wells per pad. Similar in-fills on the Pinedale Anticline had increased the total number of wells from 750 to 4,400. In the La Barge Platform, 2,940 wells had been approved, and there was currently a request to drill 1,000 more. This growth was the result of the leasing practices under President George W. Bush, which Interior Secretary Ken

FIGURE 64. These mule deer are feeding on bitterbrush and sage on their snowy winter range. Photo: Susan Marsh.

Salazar, an Obama appointee, likened to a "candy store of the oil and gas industry," where "leasing should happen almost anywhere at any cost. That's not the way it ought to be done."[14]

Another issue cited in the record of decision was air quality. The state of Wyoming requested designation of Sublette and parts of Lincoln and Sweetwater Counties as nonattainment areas for National Ambient Air Quality Standards for ozone; before the energy boom of the previous decade, these areas had had some of the cleanest air in the country. Visibility impairment was also well documented in nearby Class I areas (primarily the Bridger Wilderness). Supervisor Buchanan stated, "The potential for leasing to further contribute to impacts of elevated wintertime ozone on human health and impacts of reduced visibility on Class I areas is a key part of the rationale for my decision not to authorize leasing at this time."[15]

Wildlife-related issues included the potential for detrimental effects on Canada lynx, a threatened species that was definitely present in the Wyoming Range. "The environmental analysis underscores the importance of the lease parcels and surrounding area for virtually all aspects of the lynx life cycle,"[16] Supervisor Buchanan wrote. She also cited the continued downward trend in the mule deer population; the east slope of the Wyoming Range had provided increasingly important habitat for them as the upper Green River Basin was developed. Deer on and near Pinedale Mesa, site of the Pinedale Anticline field, had declined by 60 percent since 2001, according to research by Western Ecosystems Technology biologist Hal Sawyer.[17]

A final factor that may have influenced her decision was the large number of comments the BTNF had received on the 2010 DEIS for the PXP Eagle Prospect/Noble Basin proposal.

While many people welcomed the decision, not everyone shared their enthusiasm. The Sublette County commissioners and various industry personnel were less than pleased, and Cynthia Lummis, Wyoming's sole member in the U.S. House of Representatives, said the BTNF's decision "took into account everything but jobs, the economy, energy independence, and national security. This misguided decision puts our multiple use lands under lock and key."[18]

Four groups appealed Supervisor Buchanan's decision: Stanley Energy, Inc., Western Energy Alliance, Wold Oil Properties, Inc., and the Sublette County commissioners. In May 2011, Supervisor Buchanan decided to withdraw the January record of decision and undertake further analysis. "Withdrawing the Record of Decision will allow further evaluation of several key issues, including, but not limited to, the potential impacts to air quality, lynx habitat and mule deer migration routes. Another decision will be forthcoming,"[19] she announced. In May 2016, the BTNF updated its draft supplemental EIS to consider 39,490 acres. The preferred alternative was to withdraw consent to lease on the 30 identified parcels, in keeping with Supervisor Buchanan's original decision. The final decision is expected in January 2017.

FOR MUCH OF 2011, citizens kept an eye on both the 44,720 acres and the Eagle Prospect/Noble Basin Master Development Plan. Retired Forest supervisor Kniffy Hamilton began speaking in public about protecting the Hoback and Noble Basins. In an opinion piece in the *Casper Star-Tribune,* she wrote,

FIGURE 65. On the east slope of the Wyoming Range, the future of leases is still unresolved. Here Fish Creek Mountain looms impressively over an exploratory drill rig in the southern Wyoming Range. Photo courtesy of Mark Gocke, taken from "The Wyoming Range: Wyoming's Namesake Mountains."

As forest supervisor for more than a decade, I heard over and over the resounding public sentiment that new oil and gas development on the Bridger-Teton is not acceptable. This is not because people are opposed to oil and gas development but that other natural resource values are more important. Many of the most vocal supporters of the Wyoming Range Legacy Act were labor union members from Rock Springs and Green River who have hunted and fished and camped for generations in the southern part of the forest. Even oil and gas field workers spoke up for the Legacy Act and said that not every place should be developed. Some places—like the Bridger-Teton—are too special and too valuable to risk damaging or losing forever.[20]

The conservation coalition continued to exert pressure on the BTNF to publish a supplement to the 2010 DEIS for the 136-well proposal in Eagle Prospect/Noble Basin. Since the first DEIS had been released in 2007, the conservation coalition and others had been asking for some very basic improvements: they wanted the BTNF to produce a document that—in keeping with NEPA—was consistent with the forest plan, including all pertinent standards, guidelines, and stipulations. Any action alternative in the analysis should meet forest plan standards, and the preferred alternative should satisfy multiple objectives. As of December 2010, nothing had happened. The conservation coalition was starting to lose hope that—after yet another supplemental DEIS earlier in the year—anything useful would emerge from the process.

In December 2011, Lisa McGee met with Supervisor Buchanan to discuss this issue. In a follow-up letter, she urged the BTNF to recognize the importance of the Krug Memorandum and its stipulations. She emphasized that more than sixty years earlier, "the Upper Hoback Basin was among a limited amount of national forest acreage in Wyoming nearly withdrawn from all future oil and gas leasing. Although it was ultimately not withdrawn, citizens were promised—via this unique stipulation—that if oil and gas development were ever proposed, protection of scenic, wildlife and recreation values would be ensured in the Basin and on other select lands to which the Krug Memorandum applies."[21]

Lisa stated that no forest directives favored approval of projects based solely on their economic feasibility; on the contrary, all rights granted to PXP were "explicitly conditioned, constrained, and made subject to any and all stipulations attached to the leases."[22] In the letter, she quoted John Martini, PXP's manager of government affairs, who spoke in a radio interview in September 2011:

Issues of this nature are governed by existing laws, and I think that this point is really commonly overlooked with a lot of the dialog. . . . The Forest Service is charged with following the laws and the rules that go along with the leases of this nature when they were originally issued. . . . The question of whether drilling should occur on these leases was resolved back in 1993 when the leases were originally issued . . . and the Forest Service is charged with ensuring the most environmentally responsible project is put forward and as the applicant we respond to what they tell us the rules of the game are going to be.[23]

Toward the end of 2011, the Trust for Public Land (TPL) became involved in the effort to save the upper Hoback Basin from industrialization. Chris Deming, the TPL's project manager, explained in a long and generous interview I conducted in September 2013 how that came to pass. TWS, WOC, and CFWR had invited TPL to join their deliberations. The hard work and dedication of this group of NGOs had paid off.

Chris emphasized that the WRLA also deserved a great deal of credit for what was accomplished later because it provided a framework for permanent protection, a must for organizations or individuals who come to the table to negotiate conservation agreements. Without the WRLA, he emphasized, the TPL could not have designed anything that donors would have supported.

The TPL had been aware of the possibility of a lease buyout for several years but had determined that the time was not right to become involved. It monitored the situation until receiving a call from the conservation partners, who had decided that the TPL might be the right organization to help them negotiate a buyout. "Until it got to the point where there were serious considerations about a buyout, there was no role for us," Chris

FIGURE 66. Chris Deming of the Trust for Public Land, whose assistance was crucial in buying out the gas leases in the Hoback Basin. Photo courtesy of the Trust for Public Land.

told me. "We're not there to fight people; we are there to help find solutions."

Chris explained the differences between the TPL and other conservation organizations: the TPL does not advocate; rather, it conducts real-estate transactions to preserve natural areas. It serves as an unbiased third party like a business to find solutions for conservation priorities in communities. Private land owners, corporations, and people interested in land transactions call on the TPL, whose general mission is "conserving land for people." One advantage the TPL provided in this case is that it had previously established a cooperative and realistic working relationship with PXP in California.

Chris explained that big business operates very differently from nonprofits or the federal government. The business world is accustomed to making big deals in a very short time, whereas the TPL accomplishes its goals on a long timeline. This project possessed other challenges, not only for acquisition but—more importantly—for fund-raising and outreach. The TPL usually transfers land from private owners into conservation

protection and public ownership. One good thing here was that the USFS already owned the land and the BLM held the mineral rights. However, that meant that the TPL had to deal with the requirements of two federal agencies as well as negotiate with PXP. The TPL had to formulate a very complicated package to bring the project to fruition. Chris had queried PXP about whether it was seriously interested in a buyout and was convinced that it was anxious to reach an agreement, but the negotiations had to be kept absolutely confidential.

"We had a very short deadline to make this happen and work with industry closer than they are used to," Chris told me. "And we made the decision to do a thorough job because we felt it was in everybody's interest. Often in the real-estate world, if you're able to move fast, you are better able to make a good deal. And that was the case here."

OFTEN ON A walk along upper Hoback road, I met Dan Bailey, who frequently rode his bicycle there. He and his wife, Yvonne, had hosted the first meeting for the community with TWS and had since worked closely with the conservation community. I, like many others, was aware that negotiations were under way with PXP, and I often stopped Dan and asked how things were going. He assured me that progress was occurring and things looked promising; I should be patient and take heart. He couldn't say more than that. Since Dan had been a source of support for Dan Smitherman and CFWR since its inception, I felt I could trust his word.

WE CAN NOW return to that scene on October 5, 2012, when Susan and I had joined hundreds of others in the auditorium of Snow King Resort to await the announcement by the TPL that it had completed the buyout of PXP's leases. With Debra Love and representatives of the TPL who had

Saving a landscape too precious to drill

THE TRUST for PUBLIC LAND
CONSERVING LAND FOR PEOPLE

FIGURE 67. This postcard produced by the Trust for Public Land helped spread word about negotiating a lease buyout and raised funds to accomplish it. Photo courtesy of the Trust for Public Lands.

brokered the deal were former Governor Freudenthal, residents of the Hoback Basin, federal and state employees, ranchers, union representatives, members of the many NGOs that had participated in the process, and conservationists and sportspeople from the region. Announced as a press conference, the event felt more like a party.

During the celebration, Susan Thomas, widow of Wyoming Senator Craig Thomas, spoke about her husband, who had originally developed the framework for the WRLA. "There is no doubt that Craig believed in energy development and exploration," she said. "He also believed in special places that help give the balance that Wyoming people wanted."

Carl Bennett, a trona mine worker in Rock Springs, spoke of his hunting experiences in the Hoback since childhood, a family tradition he would now carry on with his own children. He and Mike Burd, both union members, were among those Dan Smitherman had recruited. They had become spokesmen for hunters, anglers, and campers from the Rock Springs and Green River communities who frequent the Hoback Basin.

Wyoming Governor Matt Mead also offered his support: "This story represents a respect for the valid lease rights and a respect and recognition of the value of conservation. What this is is a local idea, a local passion, that created a Wyoming cure."

JACKSON HOLE Daily

■ Regional

Exxon hit with new oil spill suit

BOZEMAN, Mont. (AP) — More than a dozen eastern Montana landowners filed a lawsuit Friday against Exxon Mobil Corp. claiming the company ignored warnings before a pipeline break that spilled an estimated 1,500 barrels of crude oil into the Yellowstone River.

The lawsuit from property owners along the scenic waterway claims last year's spill could have been avoided if Exxon followed the lead of other companies and shut down its pipeline during severe flooding in July 2011.

The 14 plaintiffs claim they suffered harm to their property and livestock operations, damage to wildlife, and health problems from exposure to oil. They are asking for unspecified compensation for their losses and punitive damages against Exxon to serve as a deterrent against future spills.

"They should have known long before this happened that this river floods every spring and produces massive erosive forces," said plaintiffs' attorney

BRADLY J. BONER/JACKSON HOLE DAILY
Susan Thomas, wife of the late Sen. Craig Thomas, R-Wyo., smiles at Carl Bennett and his daughters, Lynzie and Kami, during a press conference Friday announcing an agreement to allow a buyback of Plains Exploration and Production gas leases in the Noble Basin area of the Wyoming Range. Sen. Thomas was the original sponsor of the Wyoming Range Legacy Act, and Bennett is a trona miner from Rock Springs who opposed gas development in the Wyoming Range.

Deal stops Noble drilling

By MIKE KOSHMRL
JACKSON HOLE DAILY

Conservation groups have reached an

a look at this for several reasons," Deming said in an interview. "We've got history with these types of projects, and we have history with PXP."

PXP leases proposed 136 gas wells and 17 pads. That plan would have required 29 miles of roads, pipelines, compressor stations and other industrial infrastructure.

FIGURE 68. Susan Thomas with Wyoming Range supporter Carl Bennett and his daughters, Lynzie and Kami, at the announcement that PXP and the Trust for Public Land had reached an agreement to buy out the leases. Photo courtesy of the *Jackson Hole Daily*.

PXP had agreed to sell its leases for $8.75 million, and the agreement specified that the money had to be raised within ninety days. Philanthropists had already pledged an impressive amount. Hansjörg Wyss of the Wyss Foundation had donated $4.25 million. In a statement, he said, "I'm pleased to be able to support a practical, Wyoming solution . . . that is now a proud American legacy. This is about neighbors and communities coming together to protect an iconic Western landscape, so the Wyoming Range will always remain open for everyone to hunt, fish, hike and explore."[24]

Joe Rickets, philanthropist and rancher on the upper Hoback River, donated $1 million. Other donations came from union dues from steelworkers in Rock Springs and from workers in the Pinedale Anticline project office. One thousand individual donors raised $2 million, and Ricketts added $750,000 more to reach the final goal of $8.75 million on December 31,

2012. On Jan. 2, 2013, the TPL announced that PXP's leases had been acquired and—after due process—had been turned over to the USFS and retired—forever.

At that press conference in October, we shared a feeling of jubilation, accomplishment—and fatigue. This was a success story, but we had traveled a long and arduous journey that we hoped would not have to be repeated. The $8.75 million lease buyout was seen as a win-win business deal, a long-sought solution that respected the interests of the company as well as local sportspeople, labor groups, ranchers, and other private citizens. It was the culmination of years of work by a diverse group of Wyoming citizens who came together to prevent the development of a potentially major gas field that would have harmed wildlife and air quality and destroyed a special place.

Many people had dedicated time and energy to save the backcountry of the Wyoming Range.

FIGURE 69. Packing out of camp in the Wyoming Range after a successful elk hunt. Photo: Susan Marsh.

The result was that 1.2 million acres of national forest would be protected from further leasing and would provide a secure home range for people—ranchers, hunters, anglers, campers, hikers—and myriads of other types of life: evergreens and aspen and sagebrush and all the creatures that depend on them—greater sage grouse, northern goshawks, northern three-toed woodpeckers, great gray owls, boreal owls, grizzly and black bears, coyotes and wolves, moose, elk, mule deer, pronghorn, big horn sheep, cougars, badgers, bobcats, wolverines, Canada lynx, native cutthroat trout, Columbia spotted frogs, boreal toads, tiger salamanders, bats, Uinta ground squirrels, pocket gophers, pigmy rabbits, snowshoe hares, jackrabbits, cottontails, and a

plethora of rodents, not to mention the untold numbers of flying, crawling, and digging insects, and many more creatures in a community of "others" that share these precious acres of the Wyoming Range with humans and their horses, dogs, sheep, and cattle.

AT THE END of this conservation victory, we asked ourselves why it took so many years and such extraordinary effort. Did it have to happen this way, costing nearly $9 million and almost a decade of work by a cadre of organizations and individuals? It was touted as a market-based, win-win solution. Was it really that for everyone?

PXP had spent much time, effort, and money on the project, but we must conclude that since

FIGURE 70. Hoback Basin residents Tom and Ginger Rooks show off the banner they hung on their property along upper Hoback road. Photo: Susan Marsh.

the company was willing to consider the buyout, $8.75 million was adequate compensation. PXP deserves credit and our gratitude for agreeing to sell the leases. Was it a win-win situation for the people who live or recreate in the area? Definitely.

People contributed to the solution in their own way and at their own pace. At first, ranchers like Martha and Bill Saunders of the River Bend Ranch in Hoback Basin stood back, waiting to see what would happen. When Dan Smitherman, a well-known and respected neighbor, joined the conservation coalition, he convinced them to join the cause. "He made the difference," Martha told me. "He and all that Linda Cooper did."

Even seasonal residents got involved. Ginger and Tom Rooks allowed Dan to post a sign on their property along upper Hoback road, informing hunters about the controversy over drilling gas wells on their hunting grounds.

As a result of this communal effort, generous-spirited citizens who contributed to the outcome, as well as future residents and visitors, will go on benefiting from the clean air and water and the beautiful and healthful surroundings. The coalition of outfitters and ranchers, dependent on a healthy ecosystem for their livelihoods, will cherish the forest, as will their progeny. The leadership of Gary Amerine and CPWR paved the way for the WRLA, a noteworthy and admirable accomplishment. TU, with its reputation for effective conservation, influenced philanthropists to contribute to the buyout.

American Rivers pushed the agenda by adding the Hoback to its national list of most-endangered rivers. "The Hoback was named one of America's most endangered rivers twice—in 2011 and 2012," Scott Bosse of American Rivers told me in a September 2013 interview. "There were newspaper articles across the country, including in the *Wall Street Journal*, and all of the sudden people began hearing about this gas drilling proposal."

But it was three activists—Steff Kessler, Lisa McGee, and Dan Smitherman—with their astute timing, courage, and unflagging commitment, who brought the community and conservation organizations together in an unprecedented ecological victory for the Hoback Basin.

The philanthropists who contributed vast sums must feel rewarded when they see the way they have protected the environment. NGOs, especially the coalition of TWS, the WOC, CFWR, the GYC, and American Rivers, worked toward a common goal that kept the community informed and involved. Sensitivity to local politics and values and impeccable timing led the community through the long struggle to a successful conclusion. As Chris Wood of TU reminded us, "Conservation is an incremental process."

The late U.S. Senator Craig Thomas, U.S. Senator John Barrasso, and former Governor Dave Freudenthal remain bipartisan heroes for their essential roles in passing the WRLA and protecting the Hoback Basin. Freudenthal's courage and staying power was especially noteworthy and will be long appreciated. Saving the area from industrialization was a milestone in habitat protection for native plants and wildlife. They can now live in an undefiled natural ecosystem as they have for thousands of years.

LET'S MOVE FROM reiterating the benefits of the buyout to raising questions concerning the long and convoluted process the BTNF went through to evaluate the impact of the PXP's Eagle Prospect/Noble Basin proposal for the upper Hoback Basin. Most of those we interviewed said that NEPA—if followed faithfully—is a fair and effective way to evaluate the potential impact of development, protect ecosystems, and assure public participation in decisions. However, they also said that implementing NEPA requires much improvement; in fact, some declare it is broken. What went wrong in this case, and how can these mistakes be avoided in the future? Here are some of our observations and conclusions.

First and foremost, federal agencies should be able to withdraw areas from leasing where protection of the environment is crucial. In places where leasing is permitted, development must be reviewed and monitored to assure that environmental damage that cannot be mitigated is prohibited.

Stipulations are no substitute for a decision not to lease. The BTNF forest plan included stipulations intended to balance the need to develop energy resources against conserving forest values. The forest plan identified approximately 1.48 million acres as available for energy leasing, but a considerable amount of that was restricted by leasing stipulations and forest plan standards. As MA analyses were completed, it became increasingly clear that some parts of the forest had multiple constraints—from topography to the presence of threatened species—that made them unsuitable for development.

Had the acreage designated for leasing more closely matched what was acceptable environmentally, much less of the BTNF would have been available. This problem also surfaced in the leasing plan for the east slope of the Wyoming Range. If the BTNF had done a thorough job of identifying areas suitable for development (using the forest plan, results of environmental assessments, and changed conditions, including the 2001 roadless rule) the likely outcome would have been closer to 40,000 acres instead of 175,000.

An editorial Dan Smitherman wrote succinctly summarized the situation:

> Just think of all the time, energy and money that could have been saved if the Forest Service had made the right decision for the Hoback Basin 20 years ago. The drilling leases, which caused years of controversy, would have never been issued to begin with and $8.75 million in private donations would never have been needed. All the conflict could have been avoided.[25]

Agencies must follow the process. The TPL's Chris Deming pointed out that energy companies commonly begin with high numbers for development, expecting the governmental agency to enact restrictions, question the proposal, and define stipulations. But in the case of the Eagle Prospect/Noble Basin proposal, PXP's first drilling plan was accepted—without even a development scenario. The BTNF should have insisted upon a full-field development plan for the 2007 DEIS.

Agencies should thoroughly assess resources at risk before the time to lease. When new information emerges during development, terms need to be renegotiated. Stipulations and lease notices alone cannot forestall adverse effects. Continuous monitoring at the development site is essential.

Detailed resource inventories are needed to make good long-range land-use decisions, yet site-specific analysis is often possible only after the leases have been granted and the BLM receives the application to drill. This is a catch-22. In practice, USFS interdisciplinary teams are often told that any restriction on development is not appropriate at the leasing stage. Wait until the company submits its application to drill, team members are advised, and then apply site-specific restrictions. When the application to drill is filed and specialists then want to suggest additional restrictions to protect resources, they are told

it's too late. The company based its bid on stated stipulations, and it would not be fair to raise costs with additional constraints. This scenario played out many times in the 1990s for BTNF personnel.

Standards and stipulations cannot be ignored. In the case of the Eagle Prospect/Noble Basin project, everyone concerned assumed stipulations were in place. Forest plan requirements had been included in the original environmental analyses in the early 1990s and were supposed to be permanently attached to subsequent leases. Each decision notice that accompanied these environmental assessments included the following statement by the forest supervisor: "Based on the forest plan and this EA [environmental assessment], I am informing the BLM that we have no objection to the issuance of oil and gas leases for the lands identified as suitable in the forest plan as long as they are issued with the specified stipulations and notices."[26] Those stipulations and lease notices were outlined in each environmental assessment, and maps showed where they applied. Somehow—over the course of years and many drafts of environmental documents—they were forgotten.

The 2007 DEIS made little reference to the forest plan and none to stipulations in it. Dan Heilig, an attorney for Western Resources Advocates, spotted the omission and told the WOC and other NGOs. This error may partly explain why the BTNF received more than nineteen thousand public comments in 2007 and nearly sixty thousand comments when the 2010 DEIS was released. Respondents had had enough of the USFS downplaying potential environmental effects, failing to follow forest plan standards, and overlooking constraints such as the 2001 roadless rule.

While we may never know all the reasons why stipulations and forest plan standards were overlooked, ignored, or forgotten, it is a fact that they were intended to be essential components of a forest plan and subsequent environmental

FIGURE 71. Smoke from a forest fire cloaks the mountains above Willow Creek. A 16.2-mile section of the creek was designated a Wild River as part of the Omnibus Public Land Management Act of 2009. Photo: Susan Marsh.

documents. They are a promise, or contract, with the public and the means to implement the NFMA. If forest plan goals, standards, stipulations, and procedures had been carefully stated, integrated, followed, and supervised, many of the leases in the Wyoming Range would never have been approved to begin with.

No one interviewed for this book could tell us why stipulations were not mentioned in the 2007 DEIS, nor why none of the action alternatives met USFS requirements or forest plan standards. Everyone agreed that all parties were aware of the stipulations, so why didn't the BTNF take special care to tell the public that they would be

followed? It appears that the third-party consultants hired to write the 2007 document, as well as the BTNF staff who evaluated and approved it, ignored or overlooked them. The usual excuse was that the staff was overwhelmed with work.

Mitigation is more than a paper exercise; it must actually be accomplished. Adaptive management means shutting down operations if there are violations. Archeological resources have Section 106 of the Antiquities Act to rely on. A few wildlife species have the Endangered Species Act. Many other resources have nothing legal to protect them, only promises. When proper procedures are not followed, what recourse do agencies have? We believe that bonding must be high enough to cover mitigation costs, although, as we've shown, some damage cannot be undone.

Agencies must carefully select third-party contractors for environmental documents. Contractors frequently conduct NEPA analysis, and the developer pays for their services. As a result, the EIS moves out of the hands of the agency, and often inherent bias in the resulting environmental document downplays impacts. A more fundamental problem is the fact that a contractor can rarely duplicate the expertise of people within the agency who know the territory, procedures, and laws. Hiring a third-party contractor increases the responsibility of the agency to review and correct the report, and there is frequently inadequate time to do that. Thus, errors are perpetuated.

Although the responsibility for protecting the national forests rests with the USFS, other parties in the controversy had a duty to the public to consider sound conservation practices as part of their development strategies. The BLM, though strapped for funding and controlled by the executive branch more completely than the USFS, could have resisted the tidal wave of drilling that transformed the Green River Basin and contributed to the greater sage grouse being considered for listing under the Endangered Species Act.

Energy companies have been allowed—through lax enforcement of environmental regulations—to devastate the upper Green River Basin, one of the richest steppe habitats in the West. Recent studies demonstrate that pronghorn, usually loyal to habitat and migration routes, have faced increasing challenges from roads, fences, and natural gas fields. They may be moving more rapidly because of these obstacles and selecting lower-quality forage, with important fitness consequences.[27] Mule deer in particular have suffered alarming declines, and the prime breeding ground for the greater sage grouse has been greatly compromised. The deterioration of air and

FIGURE 72. CFWR produced this clever sticker to support saving Hoback Basin in 2011. Courtesy of Citizens for the Wyoming Range.

water quality in the upper Green River Basin also has detrimental effects on the human population.

While cash-rich energy companies help fill county coffers and build bike paths, libraries, and recreation centers, how well do they serve the community over the long term? On high-ozone winter days several years ago, the school nurse in Pinedale had to monitor air quality before children could go outside to play. Compare that to the freedom in the small grade school in Bondurant, where the children play a homemade game called "migrating elk" in their schoolyard.

The ultimate goal of energy exploration is full-field development, so the act of leasing strongly implies consent on the part of the agencies to allow ground disturbance. Citizens should also understand that the level of development considered during NEPA analysis is very likely to expand later. No matter how productive a natural gas well is when first tapped, production continually declines. Fracking only temporarily increases production. The only way to maintain production is to drill new wells. The in-fill process in the upper Green River Basin, where the number of wells is constantly increasing, is a dramatic illustration.

Responsible energy development means drilling the right place at the right pace. Rollie

Sparrowe had it right years ago: if oil and gas production had been managed in a slow, methodical, and conservative manner—the way timber was supposed to be on national forest land under the Multiple Use-Sustained Yield Act—the upper Green River Basin might not have been ruined. Rollie and others advised a slow, thoughtful approach that protected resources while developing energy. Instead, national policy favored a boom-and-bust scenario for oil, and never more so than during the late 1990s and 2000s. The goal was to get as much energy out of the ground as quickly as possible, not only for home use but foreign sales.

It takes a sustained effort by diverse interests to effect change. A wide range of citizens with different opinions and approaches combined to pass the WRLA and resist wrong place–wrong pace energy development in the BTNF. Activists working on conservation issues everywhere need to accept different points of view. Too often one approach tries to dominate, and this only creates additional strife within the community. Working together, a group of diverse citizens with a common goal protected the diverse ecosystem of the Wyoming Range.

Conservation victories are possible anywhere. The participation of local people from ranching, outfitting, and working backgrounds is what caught the attention of politicians. Raising funds largely depended on national organizations available to everyone. A few large donations certainly helped in a place like the remote Hoback Basin, where the population is small and most residents are not wealthy, but higher-population areas can raise more money from more people. Wherever people care about their environment and value their public land, they can find a way to retain what is increasingly precious. Public land—whether a national forest or state park—is a place of renewal and enjoyment, worth far more than short-term wealth.

THE EXPERIENCE OF saving the Hoback Basin from industrialization had several important results. First, it raised the environmental consciousness of the general public to the value of ecosystems like the Wyoming Range. Those directly involved learned that citizens working together can form effective coalitions and garner support from elected officials and that varied approaches usually make the issues clearer.

Perhaps most importantly, we learned that it is not wrong to begin with the impossible dream of protecting a valuable ecosystem from development. Too often groups assume there is no stopping a proposal from powerful companies and begin immediately thinking about mitigation and negotiation. A hard line for preservation is the place to start. As Mike Burd told me in our 2013 phone interview, "The Wyoming I know is gone. I don't want my kids or grandkids to say the same thing when they are my age."

This example of environmental redemption and justice—although heartening—does not address the fundamental question about changing the trajectory of government, corporations, and citizens with atavistic ideas about expansionism left over from the nineteenth century. A few decades ago, the national forests were valued as warehouses for timber. Now public land has become fair game to feed the insatiable need for energy to fuel growth—unrealistic at best in a finite world. From national policy to human activities, the watchword should be conservation: the Earth—like the Wyoming Range—has physical limits.

The Eagle Prospect/Noble Basin outcome demonstrated that good conservation practices are bipartisan and energy development is not the only legitimate use of public land. Personal recreation and renewal are also vitally important.

Today we dwell peacefully and thankfully within the Hoback Basin, mindful of what we could have lost. We will leave part of our lives

FIGURE 73. Looking downstream along the Hoback River toward Battle Mountain. At the western edge of the Hoback Basin, the river enters the canyon that bears its name. Photo: Susan Marsh.

ENERGY DEVELOPMENT OR WILDLIFE?

Can we preserve our wildlife heritage while extracting a valuable resource? Our choices will determine the balance.

The Green River Basin has been transformed to an industrial landscape through which wildlife still threads its way. Photo: Ecoflight.

The peaks of the Gros Ventre Range rise above the Hoback Basin on a spectacular fall day. Photo: Susan Marsh.

FIGURE 74. A May snowfall brightens the peaks of the Hoback Range while new aspen leaves unfurl. Photo: Susan Marsh.

here to join those who passed this way before us. We hope that our legacy enriches, rather than pollutes, the environment for others. In this way, we can continue to create an authentic culture that perpetuates our love of beauty and the land and shares them generously with the many creatures that call this place their home. We will always believe that some places are truly special. As Dan Smitherman said, "It's not only the Hoback that's too special to drill. Every place is too special to somebody."[28]

NOTES

CHAPTER 1

1. Information about BLM energy leasing in the upper Green River Basin can be found at http://www.wy.blm.gov/jio-papo/papo.
2. Emilene Ostlind, "BLM Stays Course in Wyoming Gas Patch despite Mule Deer Decline," *High Country News,* March 30, 2011, http://www.hcn.org/issues/43.5/blm-stays-course-in-wyoming-gaspatch-despite-mule-deer-decline.
3. Multiple-Use Sustained-Yield Act of 1960, Pub. L. 86-517, 74 Stat. 215 (1960); 16 U.S.C. § 1, 528n.

CHAPTER 2

1. John McPhee, *Rising from the Plains* (New York: Farrar, Straus and Giroux, 1987).
2. Robert Stuart, *The Discovery of the Oregon Trail: Robert Stuart's Narratives of his Overland Trip from Astoria in 1812–13,* ed. Philip Ashton Rollins (New York: Edward Eberstadt and Sons, 1935).
3. Arthur King Peters, *Seven Trails West* (New York: Abbeville Press, 1996).
4. Osborne Russell, *Journal of a Trapper, 1814–1892,* ed. Aubrey L. Haines (Lincoln: University of Nebraska Press, 1965).
5. Lisi Krall, *Proving Up: Domesticating Land in U.S. History* (Albany, NY: SUNY Press, 2010).
6. Susan Marsh and Rebecca Woods, *Beyond the Tetons* (Jackson: White Willow Publishing, 2010), 93–94.
7. Secretary of Agriculture James Wilson to Gifford Pinchot, February 1, 1905, http://www.fs.fed.us/greatestgood/press/mediakit/facts/pinchot.shtml. Since the letter is addressed to the Forester, Gifford Pinchot, it is generally assumed that Pinchot wrote the letter for his boss to sign.
8. Florence Rose Krall Shepard, *Sometimes Creek* (Durango, CO: Raven's Eye Press, 2012).
9. Wes Jackson, *Becoming Native to This Place* (Lexington: University Press of Kentucky, 1994).

CHAPTER 3

1. Lisi Krall, *Proving Up: Domesticating Land in U.S. History* (Albany, NY: SUNY Press, 2010).
2. Jeanne Anderson, "Carroll Noble: One of Wyoming's First Conservationists," in *Ahead of Their Time: Wyoming Voices for Wilderness,* ed. Broughton Coburn and Leila Bruno (Jackson: Wyoming Wilderness Association, 2004), 28–31.
3. Aldo Leopold, *A Sand County Almanac* (New York: Oxford University Press, 1966), xvii.
4. Julius Albert Krug, "Oil and Gas Leases in the Jackson Hole Area," Memorandum, Fed. Reg. 5859 (Aug. 30, 1947).
5. Harold K. Steen, "The Forest Service," in *Encyclopedia of American Forest and Conservation History,* ed. Richard C. Davis (New York: MacMillan, 1983) 1:243–52.
6. Dennis Roth and Frank Harmon, "Post-War Development and the Forest Service," chap. 23 in *Centennial Mini-Histories of the Forest Service,* http://www.foresthistory.org/ASPNET/Publications/centennial_minis/chap23.htm.

7. Robert Marshall quoted in Douglas W. Scott, "A Wilderness-Forever Future: A Short History of the Natural Wilderness Preservation System," 2, http://www.wilderness.net/toolboxes/documents/awareness/Doug%20Scott-A_Wilderness-Forever_Future-history.pdf.
8. Multiple-Use Sustained-Yield Act of 1960, Pub. L. 86-517, 74 Stat. 215 (1960); 16 U.S.C. § 4 a., 528n.
9. Wilderness Act of 1964, Pub. L. No. 88-577 78 Stat. 890 (1964).
10. National Environmental Policy Act of 1969, Pub. L. No. 91-190, Title I, § 101.
11. "Background Information on Wilderness and Roadless Area Evaluation," Western Forestry Leadership Coalition, http://www.wflccenter.org/news_pdf/138_pdf.pdf
12. Philip Shabecoff, "Townspeople Join to Fight Drilling," *New York Times*, September 14, 1981.

CHAPTER 4

1. Richard Heinberg, *Snake Oil: How Fracking's False Promise of Plenty Imperils Our Future* (Santa Barbara, CA: Post Carbon Institute, 2013), 4.
2. Ibid., 41–44.
3. Ann Chambers Noble, "The Jonah Field and Pinedale Anticline: A Natural-Gas Success Story," WyoHistory.org, February 2011, http://www.wyohistory.org/essays/jonah-field-and-pinedale-anticline-natural-gas-success-story.
4. Bridger-Teton National Forest, *Forest Plan,* 1990, amend. 1, pt. 3; ibid., *Oil and Gas Leasing Final Environmental Impact Statement,* 2003, sec. 1.2, pp. 1.1–1.4.
5. Kniffy Hamilton to the Wyoming state director, March 7, 2003, on file at Bridger-Teton National Forest Supervisor's Office, Jackson, WY.
6. Bridger-Teton National Forest, "Supplemental Information Report for Oil and Gas Leasing Decisions on Specific Lands in Mgt. Areas 12, 22, 23, 24, 25, 26, 31, 32, 49," February 25, 2004, copy on file with the authors.
7. Bridger-Teton National Forest, *Draft Environmental Impact Statement for Eagle Prospect,* 2007, 1–7, on file at BTNF Supervisor's Office, Jackson, WY.
8. Jim Stanford, "Forest Halts Energy Leases," *Jackson Hole News & Guide,* September 15, 2004.

CHAPTER 5

1. Bridger-Teton National Forest, *Forest Plan,* amend. 1, pt. 3, pp. 1–2.
2. Citizens Protecting the Wyoming Range, *The Wyoming Range: Too Special to Drill,* YouTube video, May 11, 2007, https://www.youtube.com/watch?v=4UqoNCwFJHg.
3. Governor Dave Freudenthal, "Comments on the Plains Exploratory Draft Environmental Impact Statement" April 30, 2007, Office of Governor Freudenthal, Cheyenne, on file at Bridger-Teton National Forest Supervisor's Office, Jackson, WY.
4. Lisa McGee on behalf of WOC, TWS, GYC, and the Jackson Hole Conservation Alliance, "Comments on the Draft Environmental Impact Statement for the Eagle Prospect/Noble Basin Exploratory Wells Project on Bridger-Teton National Forest," April 39, 2007, on file at BTNF Supervisor's Office, Jackson, WY.
5. Ibid., 50.
6. Steven Rusch, Plains Exploration & Production Company vice president, to the Bridger-Teton National Forest, June 13, 2007, on file at BTNF Supervisor's Office, Jackson, WY.
7. Greg Clark, "Bridger-Teton Begins Scoping on Plains Exploration & Production Company's Master Development Plan," press release, Bridger-Teton National Forest, December 13, 2007.
8. Lloyd Dorsey, "Wildlife Values in the Hoback Basin and Proposed PXP Site Bridger-Teton National Forest, Wyoming" (unpublished report, 2010), copy on file with the authors.
9. Gloria Flora, "Backing the Front," in *The Energy Reader,* ed. Tom Butler, Daniel Lerch, George Wuerthner, and Richard Heinberg (Sausalito, CA: Foundation for Deep Ecology, 2012), 229.
10. "Statement of Intent" in "Term Sheet: Wyoming Range Conservation & Noble Basin Development Agreement," December 10, 2010, 5.
11. Katherine Pioli, "The Buzz: No Final Agreement," *Jackson Hole Weekly,* December 15, 2010, http://www.wyomingrange.org/its-a-proposal-not-a-deal.html.
12. Cory Hatch, "Groups Criticize PXP Deal," *Jackson Hole News & Guide,* December 22, 2010.
13. Dan Smitherman quoted in Cory Hatch, "Groups Decry Drilling Plan," *Jackson Hole News & Guide,*

December 10, 2010, http:www.wyomingrange.org /citizens-for-the-wyoming-range-critical-of-forest -service-environmental-analysis.html.

CHAPTER 6

1. Dan Smitherman, e-mail message to the authors, January 5, 2011.
2. Lloyd Dorsey, "Wildlife Values in the Hoback Basin and Proposed PXP Site Bridger-Teton National Forest, Wyoming" (unpublished report, 2010), copy on file with the authors.
3. Bridger-Teton National Forest, *Forest Plan,* chap. 4, 235.
4. Ibid., 241.
5. Dorsey, "Wildlife Values in the Hoback Basin."
6. Lisa McGee, e-mail message to the authors, November 6, 2013.
7. Gregg Sherrill, "Noble Basin: A Country in the Mind," *Jackson Hole News & Guide,* March 9, 2011.
8. Cory Hatch, "Drilling Impacts Worry Governor," *Jackson Hole News & Guide*, March 15, 2011, http://www.jhnewsandguide.com/news/top _stories/drilling-impacts-worry-governor/article _34589e30-0f6f-5b22-81b2-64c02ac93341.html.
9. Cory Hatch, "New Leasing Standards," *Jackson Hole News & Guide,* September 3, 2008, http:// www.jhnewsandguide.com/news/environmental /new-leasing-standards/article_550a41b0-d5d1 -5820-9a59-0287a9367f3c.html.
10. Citizens for the Wyoming Range, "Locals Warn against Additional Leasing," press release, http:// www.wyomingrange.org.
11. Cory Hatch, "Forest to Limit Drilling," *Jackson Hole News & Guide,* January 29, 2010, http://www .jhnewsandguide.com/news/top_stories/forest -to-limit-drilling/article_bc3d18fe-5195-5b67-b3fb -5e9171894196.html.
12. Bridger-Teton National Forest, "Purpose and Need," in *Leasing in the Wyoming Range,* Final Supplemental Environmental Impact Statement, 2010, on file at Bridger-Teton National Forest Supervisor's Office, Jackson, WY.
13. Bridger-Teton National Forest, "Record of Decision," in *Oil and Gas Leasing, Wyoming Range,* 2011, 3, on file at BTNF Supervisor's Office, Jackson, WY.
14. Cory Hatch, "Interior Department Reforms Energy 'Candy Store,'" *Jackson Hole News & Guide,* January 7, 2010, http://www.jhnewsandguide.com /news/top_stories/interior-department-reforms -energy-candy-store/article_68823dcf-774b-512d -adb7-0a64efe8cf98.html.
15. Bridger-Teton National Forest, "Record of Decision," 6.
16. Ibid., 3.
17. Geoffrey O'Gara, "http://www.wyofile.com /sponsors/foundations/Deer-ly Departed: Revelation of Mule Deer 'Stop-Over' Behavior May Alter Drilling Plans in Bridger Teton Forest," *WyoFile,* May 8, 2012, http://www.wyofile.com/deer-and -drilling-revelation-of-mule-deer-stop-over-behavior -may-alter-drilling-plans-in-bridger-teton-forest/.
18. Cory Hatch, "Forest Rejects Oil, Gas Leases in Wyo. Range," *Jackson Hole News and Guide,* January 26, 2011, http://www.wyomingrange.org /forest-service-cancels-44k-leases.html.
19. Bridger-Teton National Forest, "Bridger-Teton Forest Supervisor Withdraws Decision on Wyoming Range Leases," press release, BTNF, May 5, 2011.
20. Kniffy Hamilton, "A Place too Special to Drill," *Casper Star-Tribune,* January 30, 2011, http:trib .com/news/opinion/forums/a-place-too-special -to-drill/article_2110289e-5412-540d-8b0e -632964a22d4e.html.
21. Lisa McGee, letter to Jacqueline Buchanan, December 22, 2011, on file at BTNF Supervisor's Office, Jackson, WY.
22. Ibid., 5.
23. John Martini, interview by Christie Koriakin, KHOL Radio, September 14, 2011, http:// soundcloud.com/koriakin/scene-heard-2011-09-14 -natgas.
24. Matthew Kagan, "We Did It! Hoback Drilling Leases Acquired from PXP; Lease Retirement Process Underway Thanks to Unprecedented Local Effort," press release, January 2, 2013, http://www .westernwild.org/upper-hoback-saved/.
25. Dan Smitherman, "Guest Shot" editorial, *Jackson Hole News & Guide,* May 2013.
26. Bridger-Teton National Forest, "Decision Notice and Finding of No Significant Impact," in *Making Oil and Gas Leasing Decision for Specific Lands within the Cliff Creek Management Area and Upper Hoback Management Area,* September 30, 1990, 1.

27. Renee G. Seidler, Ryan A. Long, Joel Berger, Scott Bergen, and Jon P. Beckmann, "Identifying Impediments to Long-Distance Mammal Migrations," *Conservation Biology* 29, no. 1 (February 2015): 99–109, http://ww2.coastal.edu/jjhutche/BIO370 /Extended%20abstract%20pdfs/Seidler_et_al-2015 -Con_Bio%20identifying%20impediments%20to %20long-distance%20mammal%20migrations,pdf.

28. Dan Smitherman, quoted in Kelsey Dayton, "The Accidental Activist," *WyoFile*, September 15, 2013, 4.